Family
Bike Rides

Family Bike Rides

A Guide to Over
40 Specially Selected
Bicycle Routes in
Northern California

Milton A. Grossberg

Chronicle Books
San Francisco

Edited by
Susan Weisberg
Design and typography by
Howard Jacobsen
Cartography by
Marti Somers
Photography by
Lee Foster and
Kenneth P. O'Donnell
Cover photograph by
Art Rogers

Library of Congress
Cataloging in Publication Data
Grossberg, Milton A.
Family bike rides.
1. Cycling—California—Guide-books.
2. Cycling paths—California—
Guide-books.
3. California—Description and
travel—1951-　—Guide-books.
4. Family recreation—California.
I. Title.
GV1045.5.C2G76　917.94　81-1749
ISBN 0-87701-148-6 (pbk.)　AACR2
10　9　8　7　6　5

Chronicle Books
275 Fifth Street
San Francisco, CA 94103

This book is dedicated
to my bicycling
companions Dan,
Debbie, Steve, Diane,
and faithful Rebecca.
And especially to Phyllis.

Contents

INTRODUCTION
Family Bicycling   13
  Description of Bike Paths   14
  Getting Started   15
  For More Information   16

1
Alameda County   19
  Alameda Creek   20
  Coyote Hills   22
  Lake Chabot   24
  Lake Elizabeth   25
  Lake Merritt   26
  Livermore Bikepath   28

2
Contra Costa County   31
  Contra Loma Reservoir   32
  Lafayette-Moraga Trail   34
  Lafayette Reservoir   36
  Nimitz Way   37
  Point Pinole   39
  Port Chicago Highway   40

3
Marin County   43
  Angel Island   44
  Corte Madera Creek   46
  Redwood Highway   48
  Sausalito Bikeway   49
  Stafford Lake   50
  Tiburon Bikeway   52

4
San Francisco County   55
  Golden Gate Bridge   56
  Golden Gate Park   58
  Golden Gate Promendade   60
  Lake Merced   62
  Sunset Bikeway   63

5
San Mateo County   67
  Alpine Road   68
  Bayfront Trail   70
  Canada Road   71
  Coyote Point Park   72
  Ralston Cutoff   74
  Sawyer's Camp Road   75

6

Santa Clara County 79

Alum Rock Park 80
Bol Park 82
Coyote Creek 84
Frenchman's Hill 85
Los Gatos Creek 87
Stanford University 89

7

Northern California 93

American River Parkway 95
California Aqueduct 97
Lake Tahoe Bikeway 99
Spring Lake 100
U.C. Davis 102
U.C. Santa Cruz 104
Yosemite Valley 106

Index 110

Family
Bike Rides

Family Bicycling

You are standing at the shelves of a bookstore or library, or maybe just browsing at a bicycle shop. You pick up this book, one of a row of books about favorite bike rides in Northern California. How is this book any different from all the others?

The other books describe a variety of rides, ranging from a few miles over city streets to hundreds of miles along highways and across mountains. While the authors make an effort to avoid the busiest freeways, most of their rides are along pretty trafficky roads. If you have ever driven along Coast Highway, Page Mill Road, Redwood Road, Silverado Trail, and the like, you realize that a bicyclist is at a distinct disadvantage in these places. The rides described in other books are interesting, fun, and usually over routes of great scenic beauty. They are, however, suitable for vigorous teenagers, young adults, and others in good physical shape and experienced in handling their bikes. For those of us who like to go riding with young children, they leave a lot to be desired.

Aren't there any bike routes which are fairly short, not too hilly, and, most important, completely separated from motorized traffic? The answer is, yes, there are quite a few such routes in Northern California. Until now they have never been compiled and listed in one convenient reference source.

This book describes about forty off-road, paved bicycle paths in Northern California from the ocean, across the Central Valley, to the Sierra Nevada. Most of them are concentrated in six Bay Area counties—Alameda, Contra Costa, Marin, San Francisco, San Mateo, and Santa Clara. I have personally ridden on every path described in this book. On almost all of them, I was accompanied by one or more children; on several, my wife or friends came along. So the descriptions are written from the viewpoint of family interest.

Read about the paths we've enjoyed; select those that look appealing and are conveniently located for you; then try them out. I know that you will find, as we have, that bicycling without exhaust fumes, noise, and traffic hazards is a highly pleasurable way to spend a few family hours together.

Description of Bike Paths

The description of each path begins with five features—distance, grade level, path condition, topography, and usage.

Distance is the mileage for a round trip. Where alternate routes are suggested, the mileage for each route is listed.

Grade levels classify paths in three categories, as follows:

Easy: These paths are very level. They may have some gentle ups and downs (no more than 30 feet). They can be ridden by small children or out-of-condition adults.

Moderate: These paths have either a long gradual slope or some hills of about 30 to 90 feet. They can be ridden by inexperienced riders, who may find themselves walking their bikes in places.

Difficult: These paths include steep hills of more than 90 feet. They should be ridden only by those with good bikes who have worked themselves up to this level.

It should be pointed out that all the paths in this book, even the difficult ones, would be labeled "easy" by the authors of the bicycle books mentioned above.

Path condition discusses width, smoothness, and how well the path is maintained. Most of the paths are paved all the way. A few are partially paved and partially gravel or hard-packed dirt.

Topography refers to the surroundings of the path. Some of the paths go through deep forests; some are completely open and unshaded; most fall somewhere in between these two extremes. This feature also mentions the type of scenery around each path—homes, parks, bay, fields, marshes, hills, and so on.

Usage refers to how much walking and bicycling traffic you are likely to meet. This feature is based on guess-work, since I can't be sure that I visited any path on a typical day, nor can I know whether you will take the ride on a quiet or crowded day. Still, it should provide a general idea of the traffic situation for each path. You probably won't meet anyone on those paths that are described as very lightly traveled; you probably will meet a few people on a lightly traveled path, a lot of people on a medium traveled path, a continuous stream on a heavily traveled path, and so many that your progress will be impeded on a very heavily traveled path.

The description continues with directions on how to reach the path. Many are located in parks which charge admission; wherever possible, I tell you how to get into the park legally without paying admission. Then the description concludes with

route directions, historical information, and suggestions of attractions to visit after your ride.

In these descriptions, I frequently warn you about places to be careful. These include rough pavement, narrow path, sharp curves, low clearance, road crossings, and the like. But be assured that all of the bike paths in this book are safe. As long as your group shows reasonable caution, you will be far safer on any of these paths than you would be on most on-the-street bike routes.

There is a second safety consideration which has to be discussed. Though I know of no bicyclist who has been accosted, joggers and hikers have occasionally been robbed or assaulted in various remote locations. Don't let such worries keep you from enjoying the outdoors. But please use common-sense precautions—neither children nor unaccompanied adults should venture off alone in isolated places.

To return to a happier topic, the book offers suggestions on places to take your family after the ride. These include such attractions as museums, parks, tours, amusement rides, and so on. When bicycling with children, you will probably find, as I have, that some activity after the ride will really top off your day. I haven't personally visited all of these after-the-ride attractions, so I can't be sure that you will find them all enjoyable. The location, hours, cost, and telephone number are given for each attraction. Hours and costs do change, and occasionally a facility may close entirely, so call up beforehand and avoid disappointment.

Getting Started

When you've picked out a bike path and are ready to go, take the time to tend to preliminary details before leaving home. Getting started properly can frequently make the difference between a pleasurable excursion and a disappointing one.

First, check that all bikes are in working condition. Even if your bike seems fine, pack a tool kit, which should include at least a pump, patch kit, set of tire irons, adjustable wrench, pliers, and screwdriver. Many bicyclists carry additional tools and spare parts. This is a very good idea, but most of us don't want to carry a bicycle repair shop with us wherever we go. And, as Murphy's Law tells us, the part that breaks will never be the one for which you brought a spare. On the other hand, it's a shame to abort a ride just because somebody's tire is rubbing against the fender. Your bicycle shop will have an assortment of lightweight tool sets at reasonable prices, or you can assemble your own set.

Second, pack some food, especially if you are traveling with children. A picnic is always fun on a bike ride; all of the paths in this book have pleasant, usually scenic, places to stop and eat. But even if you are planning to buy your meal, a snack during or after the ride will be well appreciated. A nice side effect of a bike trip is that kids are glad to eat nutritious food after bicycling for a while.

Finally, pack the other items you'll need: this book, of course; money; maps; a first-aid kit; and appropriate clothing. Even if it's warm when you start out, take sweaters. If you're planning to swim, don't forget swim suits and beach towels. Depending on the other activities you plan, you may also want to pack cameras, fishing equipment, binoculars, and so on.

Now that you're all prepared, how do you get to the bike path? I wish I could tell you to always take public transit, but that just isn't possible. Only a few transit systems in Northern California carry bicycles. Those that do are listed below.

The California Department of Transportation (CALTRANS) provides a commuter bicycle shuttle between San Francisco and Oakland during weekday commuter hours; telephone (415) 557-1611. Until 1978, AC Transit provided weekend "Pedal Hopper" service across the Bay Bridge, but this has been discontinued. Bicyclists can cross the Richmond–San Rafael Bridge aboard small buses operated by Traveler's Transit; telephone (415) 457-7080.

Bicyclists are allowed on BART, by permit, all hours on weekends and during noncommute hours on weekdays (9:00 A.M. to 3:30 P.M. and 6:30 P.M. to midnight). Permits are issued to people fourteen and over and to children under fourteen when accompanied by an adult. Cost is $3 per bike; the permit lasts for about three years, expiring on your birthday. BART has changed the procedure for obtaining a permit several times recently; you can now get a permit by mail. Telephone (415) 465-4100, extension 597, for the latest information.

Once you have obtained BART bicycle permits for your children, you will want to buy their train tickets at children's rates. A $6 ticket can be purchased for $1.50 for children twelve and under, but it can't be bought at stations; you must buy it at a participating bank or savings and loan office. For the location of the nearest such office, telephone (415) 465-4100, extension 569.

All Bay ferry lines allow bicycles. Golden Gate Transit has ferries from Pier 1, San Francisco (near the foot of Market Street) to Sausalito and Larkspur; telephone (415) 332-6600 in San Francisco, (415) 453-2100 in Marin County. Harbor Carriers runs ferries from Fisherman's Wharf to Angel Island and Tiburon daily during the summer and on weekends during the rest of the year, and runs a ferry from Berkeley to Angel Island on summer weekends; telephone (415) 546-2815. Angel Island State Park Ferries run from Tiburon to Angel Island daily during the summer and on weekends the rest of the year; telephone (415) 435-2131.

These are the only Northern California transit systems which allow bicycles. Unless one of these will get you to your chosen bike path, or unless you live within bicycling distance, you will have to drive there. If you drive a large van, or can fold down the rear seat of a station wagon, you may be able to carry the bicycles inside your vehicle. Most likely, you will need a bicycle carrier. A great variety of carriers for rear bumper or roof are available. Check at your bicycle, discount, or catalog store.

For More Information

The best information on bicycle paths can be obtained from the government agencies which build and maintain them. In each chapter, I have listed the addresses and phone numbers of these agencies. Contact those with information of interest to you; you will find that you are dealing with courteous, helpful public servants, not with stereotyped "faceless bureaucrats." For Marin, Alameda, and Contra Costa County cyclists, I particularly recommend obtaining the Marin County Bikeways pamphlet and the East Bay Regional Parks District (EBRPD) packet.

Bicycle clubs can also be a source of useful information on local bike routes. However, although some clubs have family bicycling programs, most of them emphasize longer distance, difficult rides. To find out about clubs in your area which meet your interests, contact:

San Francisco Bicycle Coalition
1282 7th Avenue
San Francisco, CA 94122

East Bay Bicycle Coalition
P.O. Box 1736
Oakland, CA 94604

Marin Cyclists
P.O. Box 2611
San Rafael, CA 94902

Santa Clara Valley Bicycle Association
P.O. Box 662
Los Gatos, CA 95030

Or contact your local chapter of the Sierra Club.

The national magazines *Bicycling* and *Bicycle World* rarely have any information of interest to family bicyclers. *Sunset* magazine sometimes has interesting articles on California bike routes. So does *Motorland,* the magazine of CSAA, the Northern California affiliate of the American Automobile Association.

Although I panned all those other bicycle books in my opening section, they do have interesting bike rides. If you find my rides too tame, then look up such works as:

50 Biking Holidays by Joan Jackson, Valley Publishers, Fresno, 1977.

50 Northern California Bicycle Trips by Tom Murphy, Touchstone Press, Beaverton, Oregon, 1972.

Great Bike Rides in Northern California by Thomas Ross and Carol Ross, The Ward Ritchie Press, Pasadena, 1975.

Bay Area Bikeways by Tom Standing, Ten Speed Press, Berkeley, 1972.

Bicycle books usually don't describe the plants, animals, history, or natural history of the area in very great detail. If these subjects interest you, get one of the outdoor books written primarily for walkers and hikers. Some of the best are:

Paths of Gold by Margot Patterson Doss, Chronicle Books, San Francisco, 1974.

There, There by Margot Patterson Doss, Presidio Press, San Rafael, 1978.

The East Bay Out by Malcolm Margolin, Heyday Books, Berkeley, 1974.

East Bay Trails by Bob Newey, Footloose Press, Oakland, 1975.

Discovering San Francisco Bay by Tom Tabe, The Oak Valley Press, San Mateo, 1978.

An Outdoor Guide to the San Francisco Bay Area by Dorothy L. Whitnah, Wilderness Press, Berkeley, 1976.

I particularly recommend the Margolin book for visitors interested in the ecology of EBRPD parks.

Additional historical information can be obtained from various books on local history. Some of these books cover their subject in a depth far beyond the interest of most bicyclers. However, two such books I found enjoyable are:

Discovering Marin by Louise Teather, A. Philpott, The Tamal Land Press, Fairfax, 1974.

Tickets Please by Dolan Eargle, Jr., California Living Books, San Francisco, 1979.

Information about after-the-ride attractions is available from many sources. Automobile club tourguides, such as those published by AAA and Mobil, are good references. The following books are also useful; each of them lists some places which are not listed elsewhere:

Let's Go, compiled and published by AAUW, Richmond, 1978.

Where to Take Your Children in Northern California by Davis Dutton and Tedi Pilgreen, The Ward Ritchie Press, Pasadena, 1975.

Santa Clara Valley Tourguide, compiled and published by Junior League, San Jose, 1973.

Where to Go and What to Do with the Kids in San Francisco by Mary and Richard D. Lewis, Price/Stern/Sloan Publishers, Los Angeles, 1972.

Places to Go with Children by Elizabeth Pomada, Chronicle Books, San Francisco, 1973.

1   Alameda County

The East Bay Regional Park District (EBRPD) was formed in 1934 to provide open space and recreation areas for the people of Alameda and Contra Costa Counties. Today the district operates forty parks covering over 50,000 acres. Many of the parks have good biking paths. The district will provide a free brochure on any of its parks, or for $1 will send you a complete packet, including maps and brochures on all parks in the district. Write East Bay Regional Park District; 11500 Skyline Boulevard; Oakland, CA 94619; telephone (415) 531-9300.

The city of Livermore publishes a map/brochure titled "A Pocket Guide to the Bikeways of Livermore." It may be obtained by writing to the City of Livermore; 1052 South Livermore Avenue; Livermore, CA 94550; telephone (415) 449-4000.

This chapter includes descriptions of six bicycle paths in Alameda County. They are:

1. Alameda Creek: A long, easy path along a flood control channel in Fremont and Union City (EBRPD)

2. Coyote Hills: A moderate loop between the salt ponds and marshes near Newark (EBRPD)

3. Lake Chabot: One moderate and one difficult, shady path by a scenic reservoir near Castro Valley (EBRPD)

4. Lake Elizabeth: An easy loop through Fremont's Central Park

5. Lake Merritt: An easy loop through Oakland's Lakeside Park

6. Livermore Bikepath: An easy path through an undeveloped flood plain in Livermore

Besides these six paths, there are a number of shorter paths in the county. In Fremont, there is a path along Mission Creek from Palm Avenue to Driscoll Road. In Hayward, there is a good sidewalk path along Mission Boulevard from Westchester Street to Fairway Street. San Leandro has a bayside path extending south from the end of Marina Boulevard. The

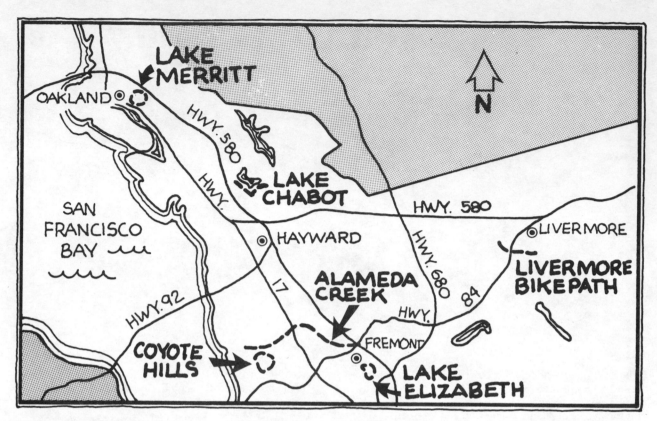

University of California at Berkeley
has a network of short paths criss-
crossing the main campus. Don
Castro Regional Park in Hayward has
a short paved path connecting to a
longer gravel path. Del Valle Regional
Park near Livermore has a paved path
from the campground to the reservoir.
And Livermore recently opened a
good 1 mile path through Sycamore
Grove Park at the south end of
Holmes Street.

Alameda Creek

Distance: 24 miles from Vallejo
Flour Mill Park to San Francisco Bay
and return

Grade Level: Easy

Path condition: Paved; wide, well
maintained, rough surface

Topography: Open; homes,
marshes, quarries, fields

Usage: Lightly traveled

This is the longest bicycle path in the
Bay Area. It offers a quiet, easy ride
through a variety of suburban and
rural scenery.

To get there, take Niles Canyon
Road east from Mission Boulevard in
the Niles district of Fremont. Take the
first right on Old Canyon Road and
then a left into an unpaved parking
lot. You will be entering a section of
the Vallejo Flour Mill Historic Park,
which marks the site of a mill built by
Jose de Jesus Vallejo in the 1850s.

Two bicycle paths leave the parking
lot. One leads to the north between
the grass-covered hills overlooking

Niles Canyon, but it lasts for only 100 yards before giving way to a dirt walking trail. So take the path going in the opposite direction, downstream.

The Alameda Creek bike trail was built in 1973 as a joint project by the U.S. Army Corps of Engineers and the Alameda County Flood Control District. It is now operated by the East Bay Regional Park District. The path parallels the creek all the way to the bay. If you want to reach the creek, you have to scramble down some rocks about 20 feet. At the start of the path, the current is quite strong; further downstream it gets sluggish. It has a good quantity of water in it for the entire length. The creek is well used by migrating birds; you may see pelicans, swans, ducks, and egrets.

The path is reasonably wide and paved, but roughly surfaced. It is very level except for thirteen underpasses which dip below roads and railroads. Near the start, you pass under Old Canyon Road, Mission Boulevard, and the Southern Pacific tracks. On your right across the creek are the older homes in the historic community of Niles. For a few years during World War I, Niles was home for the Essanay movie studios. Charlie Chaplin, Ben Turpin, Gloria Swanson, and many others made films there. If you wish to walk through Niles searching for sites associated with the movie industry, use Margot Patterson Doss's *There, There* as a guidebook.

The very large blue factory on your left is the Bernardo Water Softening Plant. You pass a large flooded quarry as the path parallels the Western Pacific tracks. You next go underneath the railroad tracks and the BART tracks. If you wait here a few minutes, you will probably see a BART train whizzing noiselessly by.

The next section of the creek is wider and deeper and much favored by birds. Near the path are a horse pasture and corral, a chard field, and another submerged quarry, which has a boat launching ramp leading down to it near the underpass at Thornton Avenue.

Beyond Thornton, the path approaches Paseo Padre Boulevard. Across Paseo Padre are some new tract homes. The other side of the creek is still open space—parks, quarries, and fields. The path is mostly sunny, but there is some shade from a wide variety of trees including acacias, peppers, locusts, pines, and eucalyptuses. The flood control district planted a line of Italian strawberry madrones all along the trail. This tree has an edible red berry which, I am told, is quite delicious.

At Decoto Boulevard, you pass a small farmyard with some goats and then more tract homes. There are posts marking the mileage to Coyote Hills every quarter-mile along this section of the path. At the 4¾ mile post, notice a path going off to the left. This is a beautifully landscaped linear park which wanders for about a mile through a new homes development. If you have time, take a side trip along it.

At this point, you are halfway to the bay, and you might wish to turn back to Niles Canyon. While the path has

Alameda Creek

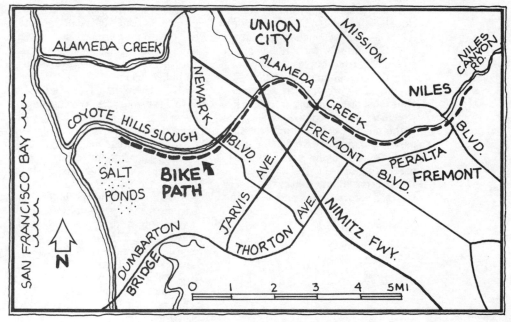

been very level, the rough surface can be tiring. If you continue, you will pass some older farmhouses, greenhouses, and cabbage fields, alternating with trailer courts and brand new tract developments. The path passes under Nimitz Freeway, Fremont Boulevard, the Southern Pacific tracks, and Newark Boulevard.

From Newark Boulevard, the path enters the marshy area approaching San Francisco Bay. On your left, you can see the Indian shell mounds in Coyote Hills Park. When the mileage markers reach zero, you approach Red Hill and a paved path cuts uphill to your left. This short path connects with the Bay View trail in Coyote Hills Park described in the next section. The Alameda Creek trail continues for another 1.5 miles past mudflats and salt ponds to the edge of the bay.

After the bike trip, you may want to ride the horse trail on the other side of the creek. The Alameda Creek Equestrian Center on Newark Boulevard in Union City rents horses. It is open daily 9–5; telephone (415) 489-2070. Or you might prefer to visit Coyote Hills Park or Fremont Central Park, which are described in other sections of this chapter. Another interesting park is Sunol Valley Regional Park above Niles Canyon. This park, also part of the East Bay Regional Park District, has hiking trails with superb views, a nature center, and an archery range. It is open daily; telephone (415) 531-9300.

Sulphur Creek Park in Hayward has hiking trails, a nature museum, and an animal lending library from which local children may actually borrow small animals for a short period. It is located at 1801 D Street; open Monday through Saturday 10–5, Sunday 12–5. Telephone (415) 881-6747.

Coyote Hills

Distance: 3.5 mile loop from Visitor Center around Bay View Trail

Grade Level: Moderate

Path condition: Paved; wide, well maintained, smooth

Topography: Open; marshes, bay, hills

Usage: Lightly traveled

Coyote Hills offers an invigorating bicycle ride through a wildlife sanctuary. Besides a scenic ride, you can have an interesting walk, or visit a nature museum or a reconstruction of an Indian village.

To get there, take Newark Boulevard west from Jarvis Avenue in Newark. After crossing the railroad track, look for the sign pointing to Coyote Hills Regional Park; it's easy to miss. Turn left and drive down Patterson Ranch Road past the truck farms to the park. Pay the entrance fee of $1 per car and continue to the parking lot by the Visitor Center.

If you object to paying $1, here is how to avoid it. Park on Newark Boulevard at the bridge over Alameda Creek just west of Patterson Ranch Road. There is room enough for two cars on the south shoulder of the road. Then take the Alameda Creek bicycle path, described in a previous section,

1.6 level miles until you join the Bay View Trail.

Coyote Hills Park was occupied for over 2500 years by Ohlone Indians. The evidence of their residence can be seen in the shell mounds they left after eating mussels and clams from the bay. The Indians departed around the turn of the century. Since then, the area has been used for dairying, truck farming, duck hunting, hang gliding, a Nike missile site, and bio-sonar marine research. Coyote Hills Park was opened to the public in 1968.

Take your bikes past the guard rail and start up the Bay View Trail on a gradual uphill. On your left is 291 foot high Red Hill; on your right are marshes. The path is very wide and smooth, with distance markers painted on the surface every 100 feet. At the crest of the path, notice a small paved trail branching downhill to the right. This leads to the Alameda Creek Trail along which our friends who parked outside are entering the park.

The path curves sharply to the left, sweeping around the north end of the hill to the bayside. When you reach the bay, you will find a concrete rack for parking bikes, a wooden observation platform, and a paved walkway leading down to the mudflats. From this spot, you can quietly view the salt ponds and appreciate the extensive bird life.

Coyote Hills is on the Pacific flyway which is the route used by birds for their annual migration. You may see red-tailed hawks, kites, pelicans, sandpipers, herons, egrets, and various other species. On one trip, I saw a beautiful male pheasant take flight only a few feet from where I was bicycling.

The path follows the bayside for just over a mile. This part of the trail has a lot of ups and downs and lefts and rights as you cling to the hillside. There is practically no foliage, only wild grasses and wild licorice. The views of the South Bay and Dumbarton Bridge are striking.

After a fairly steep climb, the path turns inland. Soon you meet a paved sidepath on your right. This is the little-used Meadowlark Trail. The Meadowlark Trail is extremely steep; the one time I took it, I had to walk my bike up a good part of it. It leads past a water district facility and police target range, to an old missile site. The site is guarded by a fence, which is sometimes locked. If it is open, you will enjoy poking among the old buildings and will have a tremendous view of the vicinity. You can check with park headquarters at the Visitor Center on whether or not the site is open before heading up the path.

The Bay View Trail forks to the left from the junction with the Meadowlark Trail and passes a day camping area and a picnic ground. At the picnic ground, the path crosses the park entrance road. Turn left and take the path which lies between the road and the marsh back to the Visitor Center. There are a number of fine walking paths and boardwalks through the tules, bulrushes, and cattails of the marsh.

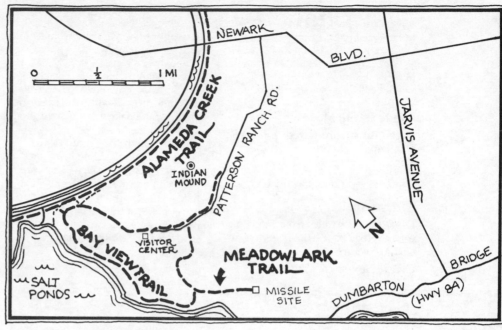

Coyote Hills

Before leaving the park, spend some time at the Visitor Center. View the natural history and Indian exhibits and the tank with local crayfish, clams, and carp. The center is open 12–4:30 on Mondays, 8:30–4:30 Tuesday through Sunday. Park naturalists have constructed a life-size Ohlone village, with summer and winter houses, a ceremonial circle, a granary, and a sweathouse at the site of one of the shell mounds. This area is open to the public by guided tours every Saturday at 2:00 P.M. and at other times by appointment. Other park activities include a nature walk through the marshes and an invigorating hike along the ridge on Red Hill Trail. Telephone park headquarters at (415) 471-4967 for more information.

An interesting activity in the area is a visit to the new San Francisco Bay Wildlife Refuge near the toll plaza of the Dumbarton Bridge. The interpretive center features exhibits, films, and lectures, as well as self-guiding nature hikes. The rangers lead walks to the ghost town of Drawbridge by arrangement. Open Wednesday through Sunday 10–5. Telephone (415) 792-0222.

Lake Chabot

EAST TRAIL

Distance: 3.5 miles from Lake Chabot Road to east end of lake and return

Grade Level: Moderate

Path condition: Paved; wide, well maintained, smooth

Topography: Shady; lake, hills

Usage: Medium to heavily traveled

WEST TRAIL

Distance: 3.0 miles from Lake Chabot Road to restricted area near dam and return

Grade Level: Difficult

Path condition: Paved; wide, not well maintained

Topography: Very shady; lake, hills

Usage: Light to medium traveled

Lake Chabot is one of the jewels of the East Bay Regional Park District. The lake offers beautiful scenery, fishing, hiking, boat rides, and two good hilly bike rides.

Lake Chabot was created in 1875 by Anthony Chabot, a noted engineer who had pioneered the hydraulic mining technique in the California goldfields. His workmen aimed gigantic water hoses at the hills and washed millions of tons of earth into San Leandro Creek. Chinese laborers spread the earth, and a team of 200 wild horses was driven back and forth to compact it into a solid mass. Over the past century, nature has repaired these indignities. The peaceful, quiet surroundings of the lake make it hard to imagine what it must have been like at its creation.

The 315 acre lake is owned by the East Bay Municipal Utility District, though its waters are used only as a standby supply in case of drought. The recreational facilities are operated by the East Bay Regional Park District, which opened Anthony Chabot Park for public use in 1966.

The entrance to the park is on Lake Chabot Road just south of the intersection with Fairmont Drive. Take either Lake Chabot Road north from Castro Valley Boulevard or Fairmont Drive east from the MacArthur Freeway (via the 150th Street exit). There is a parking fee of $1 per car, but bicyclists don't have to pay. You can park your car along Lake Chabot Road and walk down the very wide paved sidewalk path leading to the park entrance road.

Bicycle downhill to the parking lot. From the middle of the lot, you have a choice: Either follow the path straight ahead and take the east trail, or follow the path to the left and take the west trail. Perhaps you will take both of them the same day.

The east trail is the most popular. It is well maintained and has many gentle up and down grades. In the afternoon, you will find several sunny areas to stop and relax, although the path is generally well shaded. At several points along the lakeshore, there are steps leading down to wooden platforms used as boat docks and fishing piers. Almost everywhere along the path, you will have enjoyable

Lake Chabot

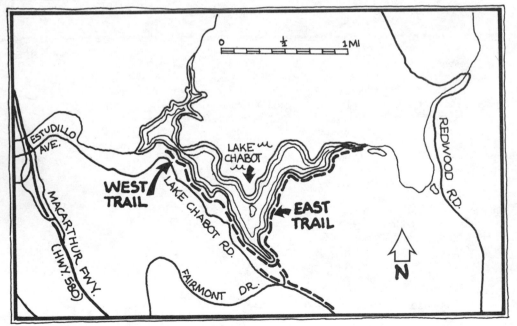

views of the lake and the surrounding hillsides covered in wild grasses and eucalyptus. There are also live oaks, buckeyes, madrones, manzanita, and elderberry trees in the vicinity.

The east trail ends at Opossum Cove, a marshy area at the southeast corner of the lake. A dirt hiking trail continues from here to the family camping area in the hills east of the lake. I suggest that you take a short walk along this trail. In about 0.2 mile, you come to an interesting wooden suspension bridge over the creek, a peaceful place to stop and relax before returning to the parking lot.

The west trail first passes the marina complex. Here you will find a snack stand and bait shop, a boat rental facility, and a tour boat. The lake is a popular fishing spot for trout, bass, crappie, bluegill, catfish, and carp. If you are age sixteen or over, you need a California fishing license plus an EBRPD permit to fish. Temporary permits may be purchased at the marina for $1.

Rental boats include rowboats, canoes, pedal boats, and electric-powered motor boats. The tour boat *Chabot Queen* leaves hourly between 11 and 4 for a 50 minute tour around the lake. You may disembark at any of four landings and return on a later trip. The *Chabot Queen* may also be chartered for private parties. Telephone the marina at (415) 881-1833, extension 36.

After passing the marina, the west trail becomes much less crowded. The path was not in great condition when my group took it, so exercise a reasonable amount of care. This path is very shady, with many live oaks and eucalyptuses. It has several good-sized hills to climb. After 1.5 miles, the path ends at the entrance to a construction site. EBMUD is building a new Chabot Dam Spillway. From this point, there are some good views of the dam and surrounding hillsides.

Anthony Chabot Regional Park extends for 6 miles north of the lake and covers 4935 acres including the lake. The park contains an equestrian center, a marksmanship range, a public golf course, an archery range, and a motorcycle trail area. Park information may be obtained by telephoning the office at (415) 531-0440.

Lake Chabot is not very far from the Oakland Zoo at Knowland Park. This is a large, well-maintained zoo with a playground, amusement rides, and a children's petting zoo. It is open Monday through Friday 10–4, weekends 10–4:30. The main zoo is free; admission to the baby zoo is 90 cents for adults, 60 cents for children; $2 per car for parking. Telephone (415) 569-7353.

Triple Pines Ranch at Kennedy Park, 19501 Hesperian Boulevard, Hayward, has a small barnyard of domestic animals with a merry-go-round, a miniature train, and pony rides. Open 11–4:30 daily in summer, weekends and holidays rest of the year. Telephone (415) 881-6700.

Lake Elizabeth

Distance: 2.7 miles from Stevenson Boulevard around the lake and return

Grade level: Easy

Path condition: Paved; wide, well maintained, smooth

Topography: Open; lake, park, fields

Usage: Varies from medium to heavily traveled

This path provides an easy bike ride with pleasant views of valley and mountains through a city park with fine facilities. The path is accessible by BART as the Fremont station is just a half-mile away.

If you go by car, take Stevenson Boulevard north from central Fremont past Civic Center Drive. There will be a road on your right marked "Police Vehicles Only" and then a dirt parking area marked "No Dumping." Park in the dirt parking area and take the paved pathway east toward the park.

The path skirts the handsomely landscaped Civic Center Building and reaches Lake Elizabeth in about 0.2 mile. This man-made lake is contained within Fremont's Central Park and covers 63 acres. The park itself covers an additional 412 acres of land. When you reach the lake, turn left to make the ride in a clockwise direction.

On your left is a large open area with roto-tilled or planted fields. There are very few trees in the vicinity, so you have extensive views of Mission Peak and the other hills of the Diablo Range. Along the path is a par course, and on the edge of the path is a variety of wildflowers.

As you round the north end of the lake, you approach the Southern

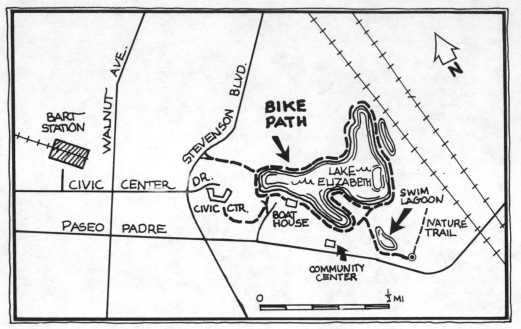

Lake Elizabeth

Pacific and Western Pacific tracks. Pedestrian underpasses beneath these tracks are used mainly by joggers and walkers seeking solitude. Continuing to the south, you find yourself on a narrow strip of land between a flood control channel and the lake. This is a marshy area with tule rushes and cattails.

Next you cross a small bridge over a sluiceway and enter the more popular part of the park. Several choices are open to you at this point. (1) To your left is the swimming lagoon with a broad sand beach. The lagoon is normally open daily during spring, summer, and fall; admission 50 cents. It is sometimes closed due to weather or crowd conditions; telephone (415) 791-4356 for information. Beyond the lagoon is a nature museum and a

boardwalk which allows you to take a self-guided nature walk into a deep marsh. (2) Straight ahead is the first of the three well-furnished playgrounds in the park. (3) To your right the path makes a long curve around a point which overlooks a wooded island.

You may wish to visit the community center with its club rooms and meeting rooms, or go on to the boathouse, where you can rent a rowboat, pedal boat, or sailboat by the hour; telephone (415) 791-4340. You can also have a picnic on the lawn or purchase food at the snack bar.

The playground to the west of the boathouse has some very distinctive climbing structures, which have led

my family to dub the park Swiss Cheese Park. From the playground, I suggest a short side trip. Go south away from the lake past the library. Then follow the path west toward the Civic Center building, where the brick plaza, articulated staircase, and landscaping are worth admiring. Then return to the playground, around the west end of the lake, and find the path leading back to Stevenson Boulevard.

After the bike ride, you may want to tour an automobile factory. General Motors in Fremont offers tours between October and June by appointment; telephone (415) 498-5500.

Mission San Jose at 43300 Mission Boulevard in Fremont has a small historical museum open daily from 10:00–4:30. There is no admission charge, but donations are accepted. Telephone (415) 656-9125.

Another possibility is Splashdown, a 50 foot high, 300 foot long water slide at 1200 Dempsey Road, Milpitas. It is open daily 9–9 during spring, summer, and fall; $2.50 per half hour. Telephone (408) 263-6961. Splashdown has no changing rooms, so come dressed in bathing suits and bring towels.

Lake Merritt

Distance: 3.8 miles from Oakland Auditorium to Rotary Science Center and return; or 3.2 miles for the loop around the lake.

Grade level: Easy

Path condition: Paved; fairly narrow, smooth

Topography: Open with some shade; lake, parks, tall buildings

Usage: Very heavily traveled

Lake Merritt is a beautiful saltwater lake in the heart of downtown Oakland. Lakeshore Park offers a great variety of interesting things to do. The bike path is short, level, and scenic, but it tends to be very crowded in places.

Parking is somewhat of a problem at Lake Merritt. I suggest parking in the lot behind the Oakland Municipal Auditorium on 10th and Fallon streets. The auditorium, built in 1914, is in the style of a classical temple. Note the bas relief sculptures on the north wall which illustrate the industries of California. The auditorium is the site of concerts, theatre, sporting events, and the like. Telephone (415) 451-7264 for a recorded schedule of events. When the auditorium is not in use, its parking lot has plenty of free parking available. Be sure to lock your car since the area is not frequently patrolled.

From the center of the north side of the auditorium, a long ramp leads down underneath 12th Street. At the end of the ramp, turn left and go up to street level. You will be at the southwest corner of Lake Merritt. This 155 acre lake was created in the 1870s by the damming of a creek flowing into the Oakland Estuary. Its creation is largely due to the efforts of Oakland Mayor Sam Merritt, for whom it was named.

Follow the sidewalk path along 12th Street, curving to the right along Lakeside Drive. Shortly after the curve, you come to the Camron-Stanford House. This handsome Italianate Victorian three-story building was built in 1876 as a private residence. Before the new Oakland

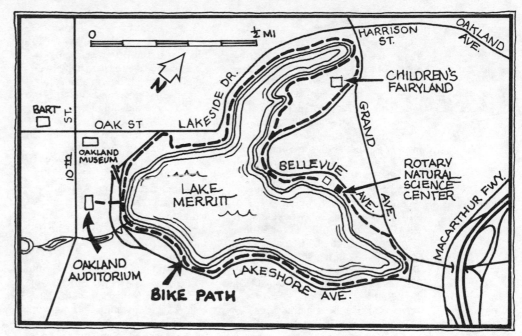

Lake Merritt

Museum was built, the museum was housed here. Today the house is operated by the Oakland Park and Recreation District, which has partially restored it. The house is open for tours and showing of historical films of old Oakland on Wednesdays 11–4 and Sundays 1–5; telephone (415) 836-1976.

Just past the Camron-Stanford House is the old boathouse, now used as headquarters for the Park and Recreation District. It is open weekdays 8:30–5; telephone (415) 273-3092. The visitor can obtain maps and brochures on the lake and its water birds.

Past the boathouse, the path curves away from the roadside and follows along the shore of the lake. The path is level, wide, and smooth, but very

crowded. The scenery is urban—clean, modern hotels and office buildings. The dominant twenty-eight-story building with the graceful curved wall is the international headquarters of Kaiser Industries. The Kaiser Center has an art exhibit on the second floor open Monday through Friday 8–5, and a roof garden open Monday through Saturday from 7:00 A.M. to 9:00 P.M., closed holidays. Both are free and visitors are welcome. Telephone (415) 271-3300.

Continuing along the shore, you soon come to the corner of the lake at Harrison and Grand. At this point, you can either continue along the shore or bear left onto the path nearer to Grand Avenue. I suggest bearing left, as the path is broader, not quite so flat, and less crowded. Also it leads to Children's Fairyland.

Children's Fairyland is an amusement park designed to delight the hearts of the younger set—say three to ten years old. There are many sets re-creating favorite storybook characters and both real and mechanical animals. The kids can slide, ride, climb, and find their way through mazes. Puppet shows are performed at 11, 2, and 4; clown shows on weekends at 11:30, 1, and 3. Fairyland is open daily 10–5:30 during summer, Wednesday through Sunday 10–5:30 during spring and fall, weekends only 10–4:30 during winter; $1 for adults, 75 cents for children. A "magic key" to unlock the talking stories costs 60 cents; there are a few kiddie rides at 25 to 40 cents each. Telephone (415) 452-2259.

Across Bellevue Avenue is the Lakeside Park Garden Center. This features a Gateway to Heaven presented to Oakland by its sister city, Fukuoka, Japan; a Polynesian garden; a cactus and succulent garden; and an herb garden. Dahlias bloom in the summer; chrysanthemums in the fall. The center is open daily from 10:00 A.M. to at least 4:00 P.M.; free.

Going downhill from Fairyland, you come to the bandstand, where concerts are held Sundays at 2:30, and a small sand beach. Next is the boathouse, which rents canoes, rowboats, pedal boats, electric boats, and sailboats. The tour boat *Merritt Queen* tours around the lake every 35 minutes; adults 50 cents, children 35 cents. Telephone (415) 444-3807.

From the boathouse, the path narrows and passes a snack bar. Just beyond is a state wildlife refuge, where thousands of ducks, geese, pelicans, gulls, and so on assemble for the 3:30 daily feeding. Nearby is the Rotary Natural Science Center, a small museum with displays of stuffed birds of all the varieties in the refuge. The science center has many live small birds, reptiles, snakes, and rodents in cages; the attendants often let kids hold the cuddlier ones. The Rotary Science Center also presents slide shows, films, and lectures. Open Tuesday through Sunday 10–5 and Monday 1–5; free. Telephone (415) 273-3739.

From here, you may turn and retrace the 1.9 miles to the auditorium. Or you can continue 1.3 miles around the east side of the lake on a fairly narrow sidewalk path along Lakeshore Avenue.

After returning to the auditorium, if you wish to ride a little further, you can turn left from the parking lot and follow a path through the somewhat run-down Peralta Park. Then cross 10th Street and follow the paved path through the campus of Laney College to its end at 7th Street.

After the ride, be sure to visit the Oakland Museum. This is a very well-organized and landscaped museum. Its exhibits cover natural science, fine arts, and the history of the land and people of California. Open Tuesday through Saturday 10–5, Sunday 12–7, closed Mondays and holidays; free. Telephone (415) 834-2413 for recorded information.

Jack London Square on the Oakland waterfront is a complex of shops and restaurants; there is also a wax museum. Still intact is Heinold's First and Last Chance Saloon, which was frequented by Jack London when he lived in Oakland.

Livermore Bikepath

Distance: 4.6 miles from Stanley and Murrieta Boulevards to east city limit and return

Grade level: Easy

Path condition: Paved; fairly narrow, smooth

Topography: Open; homes, undeveloped fields, farmland

Usage: Lightly traveled

This path is a level, lightly used trail through the flood plain of the Arroyo Mocho. Even though it goes within a few blocks of the center of the rapidly growing city of Livermore, it is still largely undeveloped and natural.

To get there, take 1st Street west from downtown Livermore. Bear right onto Stanley Boulevard, turn left at Murrieta Boulevard, and park on Murrieta as near as you can to the corner of Stanley. Walk your bikes to the west side of Murrieta just south of Stanley. You should soon see the paved path going off from the west sidewalk toward the arroyo.

The path has a few gentle grades at its start and then levels out. The flood plain is approximately a quarter-mile wide; it contains very few trees and many small bushes. It is fairly well isolated from the surrounding community, but you can still view varied architecture—older and modern apartments, newer tract homes, and older farmhouses.

At Holmes Street, the very busy State Highway 84, the path goes through an underpass. However, both times I rode here, the underpass was flooded. When this is the case, it is necessary to walk your bikes across Holmes in the crosswalk. Although this is a dangerous crossing, most drivers are courteous, and because there are stoplights nearby on Holmes, it is not too bad. Perhaps in the late summertime the underpass may have dried out enough to be usable.

East of Holmes the flood plain is much the same, except that there are a few small groves of eucalyptus and alder trees. You soon pass a development of brand new two-story single-family homes. Then the path goes through a dry and usable underpass beneath Arroyo Road.

The eastern section of the path is older and somewhat narrower. At two points, it crosses the arroyo on concrete causeways. Be very careful here, as the path can be slippery. You pass a trailer park, gravel pits, the Livermore Valley Stadium, and several farmhouses. The pavement finally ends at the Livermore city limits directly behind a Mayflower Van storage facility. Turn back here and retrace your route to Murrieta Boulevard.

After the ride, you might enjoy an outing at Shadow Cliffs Regional Recreational Area. This large hole in the ground was once a sand and gravel quarry operated by Kaiser Industries. It has been filled with water and is a popular East Bay Regional Park offering swimming, fishing, and rental boating. The park is open daily from 8:00 A.M. until dusk; parking is $1 per car on weekdays, $2 on weekends. Telephone (415) 846-3000. You can reach Shadow

Cliffs by the bicycle path that Alameda County has built along Stanley Boulevard from Murrieta Boulevard to Pleasanton. This is a sidewalk path separated from traffic by a high curb. It tends to be noisy from cars, trucks, an occasional freight train, and several quarries which are still in operation. The distance from Murrieta to the park is 3.5 miles over a pretty level stretch, with views of Mount Diablo to the north.

The Lawrence Livermore Laboratory at East Avenue and Greenville Road is a University of California facility which conducts research in the uses of nuclear energy. The visitor center features exhibits, films, and guided tours. It is open Monday through Friday 9:30–5:30, Saturdays and Sundays 12–5. Telephone (415) 422-9797. There is another Alameda County sidewalk bike path along East Avenue from the city limit at Madison Avenue to the lab (a distance of about 2 miles) if you prefer arriving by bicycle.

Livermore is wine country. Among the wineries offering tours and tasting are Concannon Vineyards, 4590 Tesla Road, (415) 447-3760; Wente Brothers, 5565 Tesla Road, (415) 447-3603; Villa Armando, 553 St. John, Pleasanton, (415) 846-5488; and Stony Ridge, 1188 Vineyard Avenue, Pleasanton, (415) 846-2133. All are open on weekends and most weekdays. In addition, you can taste cheese and view the manufacturing plant at The Cheese Factory, 830 Main Street, Pleasanton; telephone (415) 846-2577. Open daily 9–6.

Livermore Bikepath

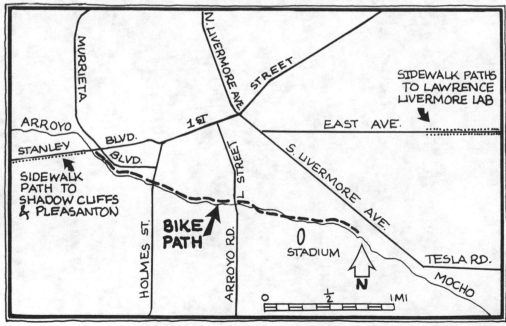

2   Contra Costa County

Many of the East Bay Regional Park District (EBRPD) parks have good biking paths. The district will provide a free brochure on any of its parks, or for $1 will send you a complete packet, including maps and brochures on all parks in the district. Write East Bay Regional Park District; 11500 Skyline Boulevard; Oakland, CA 94619; telephone (415) 531-9300.

The East Bay Municipal Utility District (EBMUD) provides water for residents of Contra Costa and Alameda counties. Several EBMUD reservoirs have bike paths. EBMUD also maintains a number of hiking trails in their remote watershed lands, for which trail use permits must be obtained at a nominal fee. Information, maps, and brochures may be obtained by writing Public Information; East Bay Municipal Utility District; 2130 Adeline Street; Oakland, CA 94623; telephone (415) 835-3000.

The city of Concord publishes a map showing bicycle routes. Write to City of Concord; Planning Department; 1950 Parkside Drive; Concord, CA 94519; telephone (415) 671-3152.

This chapter includes descriptions of six bicycle paths in Contra Costa County. They are:

1. Contra Loma Reservoir: A moderate path through open countryside south of Antioch (EBRPD)

2. Lafayette-Moraga Trail: A moderate trail between a handsome residential section of Lafayette and St. Mary's College in Moraga (EBRPD)

3. Lafayette Reservoir: A moderate loop around a scenic reservoir near Lafayette (EBMUD)

4. Nimitz Way: A moderate to difficult path along the crest of the San Pablo Ridge east of Berkeley (EBRPD)

5. Point Pinole: A moderate path through grassy meadows to the bay north of Richmond (EBRPD)

6. Port Chicago Highway: An easy to moderate path on an old railroad bed in residential Concord

Besides these six, there are several shorter paths in Contra Costa County. Two regional parks near Richmond—

George Miller, Jr., and Point Isabel—have short paved bicycle paths. Briones Regional Park has a very hilly dirt road which has been closed to motorized traffic. In Walnut Creek, there is a good sidewalk path along Ygnacio Valley Road for a mile to the east from Heather Farms Park. And Old San Pablo Road is a 5 mile long, hilly, paved road closed to automobile traffic along the west shore of San Pablo Reservoir. At the time of writing, EBMUD is performing construction work here and has closed the path; it is supposed to reopen sometime in 1981.

Contra Loma Reservoir

Distance: 4.6 miles from Lone Tree Way to Contra Loma swimming beach and return

Grade level: Moderate, except for one difficult hill

Path condition: Paved; wide and smooth most of the way, but one very rough section

Topography: Open; some homes, fields, canal, reservoir

Usage: Lightly traveled

This ride starts as a quiet, gentle jaunt along a scenic semiresidential route; proceeds over some easy hills; and then has a very steep climb. The climbing effort is well rewarded, however, for you can finish your ride with a cool swim in Contra Loma Reservoir.

To get to the path, drive south on Lone Tree Way from Highway 4 in Antioch. Just past the intersection of Clayburn Road, you come to the

Contra Costa County

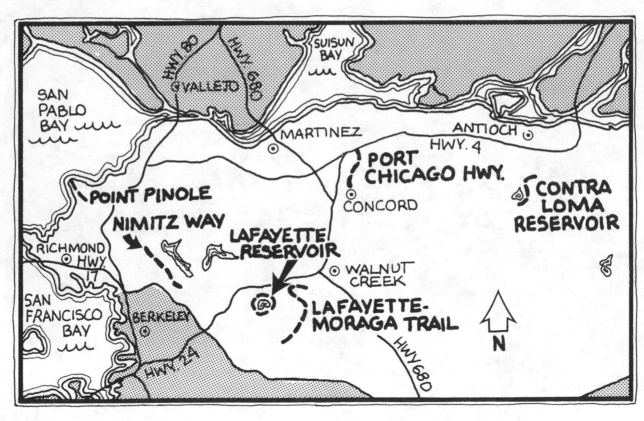

Contra Costa Canal. Park on the shoulder of Lone Tree Way, and start bicycling on the path which follows the north edge of the canal.

The path is wide and smooth. It starts out level but soon goes up and down some small hills. On your right is a broad flood plain and beyond that some new homes. On your left, across the narrow fenced-in canal, is the earthen retaining wall of the Antioch Municipal Reservoir. From time to time, you have good views of Antioch, the San Joaquin River, Antioch Bridge, and Mount Diablo.

After making a sharp right turn, the path and canal parallel a newly built street, Paso Corto Road. Across the street is a brand new tract of single-family homes. This section of the path is again very level. Like most of the path, it is virtually treeless; there are some wild grasses and wildflowers in the area.

Soon you will see a sign pointing to Contra Loma Regional Park. Cross the canal on a little concrete bridge and follow the path through an almond orchard. Open the wooden gate into the cow pasture, and, if you are as lucky as we were when we made this trip, you'll see a herd of cows blocking the path and staring at you. We found that you can make a cow move by looking it straight in the eye and saying in a firm voice, "Move, cow." It's not the authentic Western way of doing it, but it seems to work.

At the edge of the pasture, you come to a fork. The path to the right goes toward the restricted Water District area at the foot of the dam. Take the path on the left. This climbs 110 feet up a very steep hill. Unless you are in excellent shape and have a good ten-speed, plan to walk your bike up this hill.

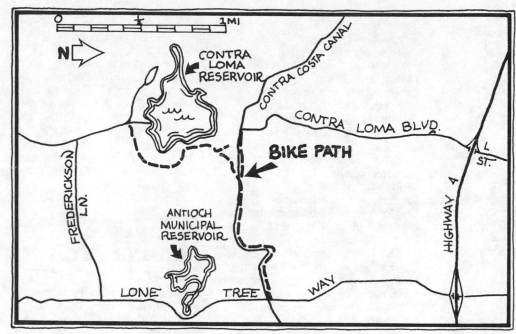

Contra Loma Reservoir

At the top of the hill is a gate with a padlock. When my family first saw the padlock, we started cursing the cruel people who had so effectively prevented us from getting through. Soon, however, a man on a bicycle with a dog running alongside came up, greeted us courteously, and showed us the walker's gate on the side of the padlocked barrier. We chatted with him for a minute; he was the owner of the cows grazing below. The gate arrangement is designed to let bicyclists, walkers, and park ranger vehicles through, while banning access to cattle. So if you are more dexterous than, and at least as smart as, the average cow, you should have little difficulty in getting through this formidable barrier.

You are now within the confines of Contra Loma Regional Park, riding on a wide and paved, though poorly maintained, fire road. There is a lot of loose gravel on the road, so be careful as you go down the grade. On your right is the cool blue reservoir. Around you are grassy hillsides teeming with small birds and a very few oak and olive trees.

At the south end of the reservoir, the fire road meets the main park road near the boat launching ramp. Turn left and then quickly right and walk or ride 0.2 mile to the main parking lot. At the recreation area nearby, you will find grassy lawns, picnic tables, the swimming beach, showers and changing rooms, and a food concession. The swimming beach is open daily 11–6, from about May 1 to October 1; free. Telephone (415) 757-0404.

Fishermen can catch rainbow trout, catfish, bass, crappie, bluegill, and sunfish. Bait, fishing supplies, and fishing permits (required for people over sixteen) are sold at the concession. The park has some fine uncrowded hiking trails through the grassy hills. Parking is $1 per car on weekdays, $2 on weekends; bicyclists, of course, can park for free.

Black Diamond Mines Regional Preserve on the north slope of Mt. Diablo was a major coal and sand mining area from 1855 until 1949. The East Bay Regional Park District has rehabilitated several of the mine openings and allows public access to them. Some of the sites require a tourguide and advance reservations; charge for adults is $1, for those eighteen and under 50 cents. Telephone (415) 757-2620. There is a hiking trail from Contra Loma Park to the Black Diamond Preserve, but it leads to a remote section of the preserve. To get to the main part, you will need to return to your car and drive south from Antioch on Somersville Drive.

Another interesting attraction in the area is the California Railway Museum located on Highway 12 between Rio Vista and Fairfield. There is a fine collection of old trains, trolleys, and cable cars, plus a museum of streetcar memorabilia. The museum has a number of restored cars including some Key System cars, a Sacramento Northern trolley, an open Liverpool tram, and many others. Admission is $3 for adults, $2 for ages twelve–seventeen, $1 for ages three–eleven, and includes as many streetcar rides as you like. Open Saturday, Sunday, and holidays 12–5, weather permitting. Telephone (707) 374-2978.

If old mines or railroad cars don't appeal to you, you might want to end your day at Brannan Island State Recreation Area. It is on Highway 160, 4 miles south of Rio Vista. The area has picnic sites, a swimming beach, camping, and a boat-launching area; lifeguards are on duty during summer. Open daily; parking $2. Telephone (916) 777-6671.

Lafayette-Moraga Trail

Distance: 11.6 miles from Olympic Boulevard and Reliez Station Road to St. Mary's Road and Moraga Road and return

Grade level: Moderate

Path condition: Paved; fairly wide, smooth, well maintained

Topography: Generally shady; homes, schools, creek, grassy hillsides

Usage: Medium traveled

This path provides an interesting contrast between the highly developed attractive residential neighborhoods in Lafayette and the open grazing lands in Moraga. It also gives you an almost painless way to make a 400 foot climb. Because the path is built on an old railroad right-of-way, the grade is so gradual that you won't realize how high you are climbing.

Get to this path by taking Pleasant Hill Road south from Highway 24. Turn right at the end of Pleasant Hill on to Olympic Boulevard. Olympic ends at Reliez Station Road; park in the small dirt parking lot at the corner. The bike trail starts on the west side of Reliez Station as a continuation of Olympic Boulevard.

The Lafayette-Moraga Trail is built on an abandoned line of the Sacramento Northern Railroad, which once provided passenger service between Oakland and Sacramento. The trail was opened by the East Bay Regional Park District in 1976. The district has erected large woodcut signs at the start of the trail and at several points along it describing the trail and warning the user against poison oak.

The trail goes through an attractive residential section as it heads to the west. On both sides are the backyards of single-family homes. There is a good deal of shade from a variety of trees, including acacia, oak, walnut, buckeye, pine, fir, maple, and eucalyptus. The pavement has a number of expansion cracks which have been filled in and is generally well maintained.

As you ride through Lafayette, you will be annoyed by the barriers at about a dozen cross streets. They are wide enough for a single bicyclist to pass without dismounting, but it is necessary to slow down almost to a stop to get through safely. They will be even more of a nuisance on the way back, when you are speeding down the slope. However, if you remember that they are there to discourage motorized vehicles and that they do so effectively, you will realize that they enhance your biking pleasure more than they detract from it.

At Las Trampas School, the path cuts through the parking lot and goes uphill past a water district facility and over a bridge high above Las Trampas Creek. Now you have rounded the ridge and are coming back in a southeasterly direction. You are still in a residential district, but you will see an occasional apricot orchard among the homes.

After crossing the creek again on a natural wooden bridge, you enter some open fields with views of the surrounding hills. You soon cross St. Mary's Road and enter Moraga. The scenery changes dramatically. The trail goes through an oak and chapparal forest about 50 feet away from St. Mary's Road. You will see a large number of wild artichoke plants along the path, and cattle grazing on the nearby hills. Soon you pass a single picnic table in a wooden shelter set in an oak grove.

The one steep slope on the path occurs as you approach Rheem Boulevard. This is about a 60 foot climb in 0.1 mile. After crossing Rheem, the path levels out. St. Mary's College appears across St. Mary's Road; cross the road and explore the beautiful campus.

St. Mary's College was founded in San Francisco by Archbishop Alemany in 1863. It moved first to Oakland and then, in 1928, to Moraga. It is now a coeducational college with 1500 students operated by the Christian Brothers. The buildings are in the Spanish Mission style, with red tiled roofs. The campus is dominated by a beautiful Baroque-style church from whose bell tower lovely music is played hourly.

After leaving the college, the path continues on a downhill slope. You go

through a par course situated in an abandoned orchard. The path officially ends at the corner of St. Mary's Road and Moraga Road. There is a paved asphalt path extending up Moraga Road for about a half-mile toward Rheem Valley. You may take this path and continue biking, stop here and explore nearby Moraga Village, or immediately turn back to Lafayette.

After the ride, you might like to visit Redwood Regional Park, a few miles west of Moraga. The park has hiking trails, picnicking, an archery range, playing fields, a children's play area, a wading pool, a swimming pool with changing rooms, and fine groves of coast redwoods. Parking is $1 per

car on weekdays and $2 on weekends; swimming is $1 for adults and 25 cents for children under twelve. The park is open daily during daylight hours. The pools are open daily May 1 to Labor Day, and then on weekends until the end of October. Telephone (415) 531-9280.

To the east is Mount Diablo State Park. This 7919 acre park encompasses the famous East Bay mountain landmark. It has some great hiking, unsurpassed views (on clear days), picnicking, overnight camping, a small museum run by volunteers which is generally open on weekends, and a ranger program. The park is open daily during daylight hours; entrance fee is $2 per car. Telephone (415) 837-2525.

Lafayette-Moraga Trail

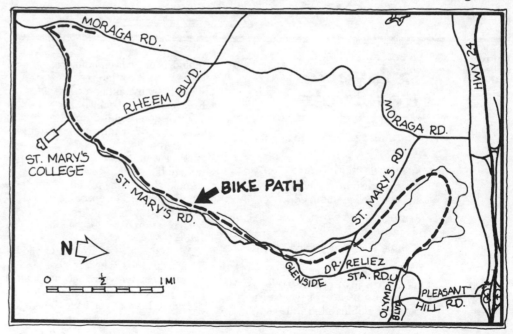

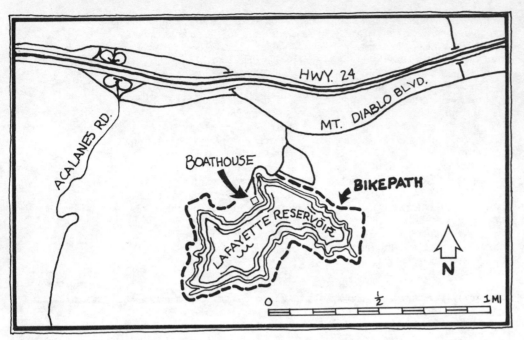

Lafayette Reservoir

Distance: 2.7 mile loop around reservoir

Grade level: Moderate

Path condition: Paved; fairly wide, smooth, well maintained

Topography: Open; reservoir, hills, chapparal

Usage: Heavily traveled

This trail is a very popular one and well worth an afternoon's ride. The reservoir is in a very scenic area—a peaceful, uninhabited valley surrounded by the populous suburbs of west Contra Costa County. The path, though short, has enough ups and downs to make it interesting.

Get there by taking the Acalanes Road exit south from Highway 24. Turn east on Mount Diablo Boulevard, and go one mile to the entrance road to the reservoir. Many people park on Mount Diablo Boulevard and walk or bike in. However, I strongly recommend driving in and paying the admission fee. The entrance road is very steep, narrow, and trafficky; it is not a pleasant place for walking or riding bicycles.

Admission is $1 on weekdays and $2 on weekends. There is a coin-operated barrier which accepts quarters. A dollar bill changer is also provided. Be sure you have the proper change, as the barrier is usually unattended. The reservoir is open daily from sunrise to sunset. Telephone (415) 284-9669.

The main parking lot is located about 0.2 mile to the right of the barrier, directly above the boathouse. Sometimes when there is a large crowd, cars are allowed to park in the grassy area on top of the dam. At the boathouse, you can purchase fishing equipment and licenses, buy snacks, rent boats, or pick up a free leaflet describing the reservoir. There are also a small fish tank containing some of the species found in the lake and a few nature exhibits.

Start the bike ride from the main parking lot above the boathouse. You will ride around the lake in a counter-clockwise direction. The path is smooth and well maintained. There is very little shade—only a few oaks, willows, and cottonwoods near the shore and a lot of coyote bush, thistles, and wildflowers on the hillsides. The reservoir is in a large natural bowl surrounded by grassy hills. As a result, there is very little wind and very little evidence of the residential area on the other side of the hills.

The path starts out on a level course, but you soon come to a series of ups and downs—roller coasters, as my children have named them. The grades are so short and steep that, if you do it properly, you can gain enough momentum on each downslope to carry you up the succeeding upslope.

As you circle the lake, you will notice a number of picnic tables, restrooms, and floating fishing docks scattered around the shore. The California Department of Fish and Game stocks the lake with trout; the reservoir also contains bluegill, black bass, crappie, and catfish. Normal state limits and license requirements apply.

Lafayette Reservoir was built by the East Bay Municipal Water District in the mid-1920s. It was originally intended to be a much larger reservoir, but in 1928 the earth beneath the dam settled, and huge cracks appeared. The citizens of Lafayette became understandably nervous, so EBMUD widened the dam and reduced the size of the lake. The intake tower which now rises high above the surface shows how deep the lake was supposed to be. Today the 115 acre lake is used as an emergency water supply for EBMUD customers.

As you approach the eastern side of the reservoir, the hills become steeper, and you may have to walk your bikes up some of them. On the northeast corner is a grassy area used for group picnics; there are also a number of Monterey pines planted shortly after the construction of the dam.

When you get to the dam, stay to the left and cross it on the partly paved–partly graveled road. Then take the access road down toward the boathouse and up the steep hill to the parking lot and your car.

The nearby Alexander Lindsay Junior Museum at 1901 First Avenue in Larkey Park, Walnut Creek, has a collection of caged animals. These are mostly small native animals, including some that children can hold. The museum is open Tuesday through Friday 1–5, Saturday and holidays 11–3, closed Sunday and Monday; free. Telephone (415) 935-1978. Larkey Park has a swimming pool open Monday through Friday 3–5, weekends 12–5; adults $1, children seven to eighteen, 75 cents, under seven free. Telephone (415) 939-1532. Also in the park is the clubhouse of the Walnut Creek Model Railroaders, with an elaborate, detailed layout. It is open to the public from 8:00 to 10:00 P.M. on the last Friday of each month and on the weekends before and after Thanksgiving; the club also has a Sunday show about once every two months. Entrance fee for adults is $1, children six to twelve 25 cents, under six free. Telephone (415) 937-1888.

Briones Regional Park on Bear Creek Road has archery, hiking, a children's environmental play area, several unpaved bike trails, and a self-guiding nature trail. At the north entrance to the park on Alhambra Valley Road, there is a wildflower nature trail. This trail is guided by the Briones Wildflower Kit, available at libraries in Orinda, Concord, Pleasant Hill, Martinez, Walnut Creek, and Lafayette. A $5 deposit is required for the kit; overdue fine is $1 per day. Telephone (415) 229-3020.

Nimitz Way

Distance: 8.2 miles from Inspiration Point to Nike missile site and return

Grade level: Moderate to difficult

Path condition: Paved; wide, smooth, well maintained

Topography: Partly shaded, partly open; hills, park, long views

Usage: Heavily traveled near Inspiration Point; lightly traveled near missile site

Nimitz Way is a paved road which was used as access to a military base in the years after World War II. It is now closed to motor vehicles and offers a fairly long, hilly ride with some beautiful views.

If coming from the south, drive north on Camino Pablo from Highway 24 in Orinda. Turn left on Wildcat Canyon Road to Inspiration Point. If coming from the north, get to Grizzly Peak Boulevard in Berkeley. Then take Shasta Road into Tilden Park and follow Wildcat Canyon Road across the park to Inspiration Point. There is a large circular parking area at the point. Walk your bikes around the barrier at the west end of the parking lot onto Nimitz Way.

The road is quite wide and starts out with a slight upgrade. This is just the first of many rolling hills you will encounter. The road alternately climbs and drops, usually 40 feet or less at a time. This first part of the path is extremely popular with walkers and joggers, so be careful. They will soon thin out.

The path follows the line of the San Pablo Ridge. On your left are the hills, lawns, and forests of Tilden Park. On your right, the grass- and chapparal-covered hills slope down to San Pablo Reservoir. You will pass a few groves of trees—eucalyptus, pine, madrone, live oak and buckeye—but for the most part you will be in open space.

After about 2 miles, you climb a higher hill (about 60 feet) and come to a T intersection. Nimitz Way continues to the right. The road to the left goes steeply uphill for 0.4 mile and then ends. It is an access road for the military reservation which was formerly located here. The intersection is a good quiet place to rest; the cattle grazing in the area won't mind sharing their scenic hillside with you.

Continuing north, you enter Wildcat Canyon Regional Park. Wildcat Canyon, like Tilden, is a part of the

East Bay Regional Park District; however, it has very different characteristics. While Tilden is a long-established park (1935) with many fine facilities, Wildcat Canyon was only formed in 1976. It is mostly undeveloped, with some fine hiking trails. You are likely to see relatively few people here, but you may see redtail hawks, kestrels, or turkey vultures gliding on air currents.

This section of the path is a long, very gradual, downhill slope until you get to the 3.7 mile point (mileages are marked on the roadway every tenth of a mile). Then you climb a very steep hill, 140 feet in a quarter-mile. Here the path circles around the hill on which the old Nike missile site was located. Be sure to leave your bikes and climb an additional 30 feet to the

crest. You will be rewarded with beautiful 360-degree views of San Pablo Dam, El Sobrante, San Pablo Bay, Richmond, and Wildcat Canyon. All that is left of the missile site itself are the foundations of the missile launchers and silos. Incidentally, if you are interested in seeing how such a site operated, the Golden Gate National Recreation Area has tours at Fort Cronkhite. See the section on the Golden Gate Bridge (in Chapter 4) for more information.

From the missile site, the Clark-Boas trail, which is unpaved, continues to the north along the ridge line for another four miles, gradually descending to end near San Pablo Dam Road in El Sobrante. While some bicyclists use this trail, I suggest you turn around at the missile site and take Nimitz Way back to

Inspiration Point, unless you're in the mood for a long, bumpy, dusty ride.

A tremendous variety of after-the-ride family activities can be enjoyed in Tilden Park. Lake Anza has a concession stand, picnic area, and swimming beach with lifeguards on duty 11–6 daily from about May 15 to September 30. Swim fees are $1 for adults and 25 cents for children twelve and under.

At Jewel Lake, there is a nature area with a boardwalk, self-guiding nature trail, and the Little Farm, where many domestic animals may be petted and fed. The Little Farm is open daily 8–4:30. The Environmental Education Center at Jewel Lake has some displays and presents interpretive programs. It is open Tuesday through Sunday 10–5. Telephone (415) 525-2233.

The Tilden Park merry-go-round is an antique carousel in the woods. A great favorite with the kids, it costs 30 cents a ride. There is also a miniature steam railroad at the south entrance which costs 50 cents a ride. Pony rides at Canon Drive near the Spruce Gate entrance cost 50 cents. All rides operate daily during the summer and on weekends during the rest of the year; 10–5 for the merry-go-round and pony ride, 11–6 for the little train.

The Botanic Garden has a fine collection of native plants. It is open daily 10–5; 75 cents for adults, 50 cents for students, 25 cents for children twelve and under. Tilden Park also has a miniature airplane field and a public golf course. Telephone EBRPD Headquarters at (415) 531-9300 for further information.

Nimitz Way

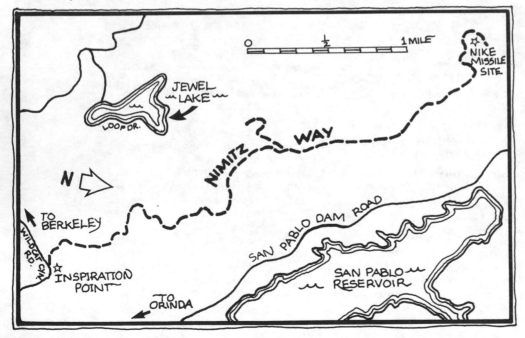

When you finally leave Tilden Park, consider stopping at the Lawrence Hall of Science at Canyon Road North and Centennial Drive in Berkeley. This excellent science museum has many exhibits in mathematics, astronomy, electronics, mechanics, and biology. Many of the displays allow user participation. It is open Monday through Friday 10–4:30, Saturday and Sunday 10–5. Fee for adults is $2.50, students $1.50, children twelve and under $1; computer game playing on a first-come, first-served basis at $1.50 per half-hour. Telephone (415) 642-5132.

Point Pinole

Distance: 3.2 miles from parking area to fishing pier and return

Grade level: Moderate

Path condition: Paved; wide, smooth, well maintained

Topography: Partly shaded, partly open; meadows, eucalyptus groves, bay, marshes

Usage: Medium traveled

Point Pinole was closed to the public for almost a hundred years until its opening by the East Bay Regional Park District in 1971. From the 1880s to the 1960s a succession of gunpowder manufacturers—Safety, Nitro, Atlas, and Giant—occupied the peninsula, making dynamite and nitroglycerine in a multitude of small buildings spread out over the area. To guard against an explosion, elaborate precautions were used. Employees were searched daily for matches or for any metal article that could cause a spark. The narrow-gauge railway that serviced the plant was battery operated and ran on wooden rails. Each day's production was packed in aluminum crates, sealed in paraffin, and shipped out that same day on barges. These precautions were successful; the Pinole companies never had a serious accident.

In 1963, Atlas closed the factory and sold the land to Bethlehem Steel Company, which planned to build an addition to its large galvanizing plant on Atlas Road. After years of environmental agitation, Bethlehem sold Point Pinole to the Park District. In 1971, the park was finally opened to the public.

Because of the unusual way the land had been used, it escaped the ravages of overdevelopment suffered by most of its surroundings. Today it is a delightful place. Gently rolling hills are covered with grassy meadows dotted with groves of blue gum eucalyptus. Near the bay are high cliffs, sand beaches, and saltwater marshes, a favorite resting spot for many birds traveling the Pacific flyway.

You can get to the park by taking Hilltop Drive west from Interstate 80. Turn right on San Pablo Avenue for about 1 mile, then left on Atlas Road. Follow Atlas until it makes a 90-degree left turn and becomes Giant Highway. Look for the park entrance on your right.

Admission to the Point Pinole parking lot is $1 per car on weekends. You

Point Pinole

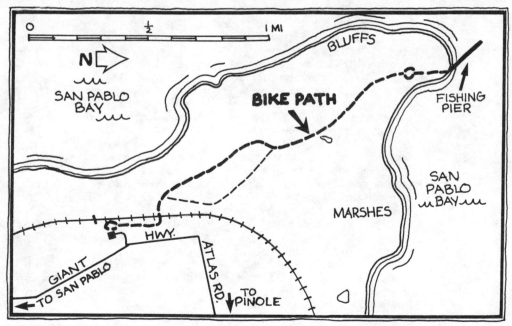

can avoid this fee by parking on the shoulder of Giant and walking your bikes in. Continue downhill past the entrance station, through the barrier gate, to the rotary used by the park shuttle bus to the fishing pier. Shuttle service consists of a pickup truck which pulls from one to three open-sided trailer cars. Each car can carry about twenty-five passengers, who store their fishing gear in the back of the truck. The shuttle makes a round trip once an hour, at a cost of 25 cents per person each way. Telephone (415) 237-6896 for park information.

Bicycle up the grade which parallels the railroad tracks and cross the concrete bridge over the tracks. You will be crossing the Southern Pacific tracks used by freight and Amtrak passenger trains. The path, which is actually a smooth road used by the park shuttle, continues uphill. It is mostly unshaded, as it goes through grassy meadows, and is usually crowded with walkers.

A short distance past the bridge, you will come to a side road forking off to the right. You will enjoy taking this alternate road either on the way out or on your return trip. It passes through a cool, deep eucalyptus grove, skirts the foundation of one of the former powder factories, goes through a meadow covered with wild-flowers, and then rejoins the main path near the crest of the hill. The side path is paved, but the pavement is in poor condition, so be careful. Unlike the crowded main path, this side path is usually deserted.

From the crest, there is a long gentle downgrade past a freshwater pond and to the rotary where the shuttle bus ends its route. At this rotary are water, restrooms, picnic

tables, and an earthen bulwark that was used for storing explosives. A paved path continues for another tenth of a mile to the 1225 foot long concrete pier. A fishing license is not required for fishing from the pier. It is usually crowded with people trying to catch salmon, trout, sturgeon, and bass.

Before returning to the parking lot, you might want to go for a walk. The bluffs path, leading south from the point along the cliffs and the beach, follows the route of the old railway; some of the old munitions storage batteries and factory sites can be seen. Another interesting walk is along the marsh path. This path cuts east from the shuttle rotary, skirting a pickle-weed marsh. It is a favorite of bird watchers. All of the side paths are very isolated; it is not a good idea to let children go off on them alone.

The nearby Castro Point Railway Museum is a club-owned museum of full-size locomotives and rolling stock. Free rides on a steam-powered train are offered on the first Sunday of each month, weather permitting. The museum is located at Point Molate, the last Richmond exit before the Richmond–San Rafael Bridge. The museum is open weekends; admission is free, but donations are gladly received. Telephone (415) 234-6473 or (415) 643-0354.

The Richmond Museum at 3510 Cutting Boulevard offers displays on local history and Indian culture. At present, the museum does not have regular hours; it is open by appointment; telephone (415) 235-7387. By the time this book is published, the museum should be open regularly.

Port Chicago Highway

Distance: 3.8 miles from Port Chicago Highway and Bonifacio Street to Highway 4 and return

Grade level: Easy to moderate

Path condition: Paved; wide, smooth, not well maintained

Topography: Open; homes, park, military reservation

Usage: Lightly traveled

This is an easy bike ride through a residential section of Concord. It is built on an abandoned right-of-way of the Sacramento Northern Railroad, which provided interurban service on electrified trolleys between Oakland and Sacramento until about 1941. You can still ride on one of the restored Sacramento Northern trolleys at the California Railway Museum near Fairfield. This museum is described in the section on the Contra Loma bike path.

Park at the corner of Bonifacio Street and Port Chicago Highway a few blocks northeast of downtown Concord. Cross over to the northeast corner and start bicycling on the path, which parallels Port Chicago Highway.

The path immediately swings through Baldwin Park, a small, well-landscaped city park with picnic tables, barbecue pits, and playing fields. After one block, the path exits from the park and returns to the side of the road just across the street from Mount Diablo Hospital.

The path is very wide, smooth asphalt. It is edged with gravel which sometimes gets on the path, so be careful. The path is fairly level with a few gentle ups and downs. The city has planted some young trees, but they provide little shade. On your left, the roadside is about 20 feet away; on your right is a redwood fence separating you from a row of homes.

At 6th Street, you must dismount, walk your bike past a barrier, cross at the stoplight, walk through another barrier, and then remount. You have to go through the same rigamarole at Olivera Street. At Olivera you could make a side trip of 0.6 mile east by sidewalk and street to Pixie Playland. This attraction is discussed below.

From Olivera Street, the path slopes uphill in a long but gentle grade. Across the street on your left are some hillside homes. On your right, behind a chainlink fence topped with barbed wire, is the Concord Naval Weapons Station. About all you can see of the station are grassy fields and stately palm trees. At the top of the hill, you look down on a narrow green valley through the middle of which the Antioch Freeway, Route 4, runs. The bike path ends here. After relaxing for a while, return to Bonifacio Street.

The right-of-way continues south from Bonifacio to the Concord BART Station, but this section is covered with loose gravel and is not suitable for bicycle riding. Concord has posted an on-street bicycle route through downtown to the station. From this station, there is a pleasant paved bike path going south for 0.5 mile. This path follows the landscaped linear park directly under the BART tracks from Mount Diablo Street to Galindo Creek.

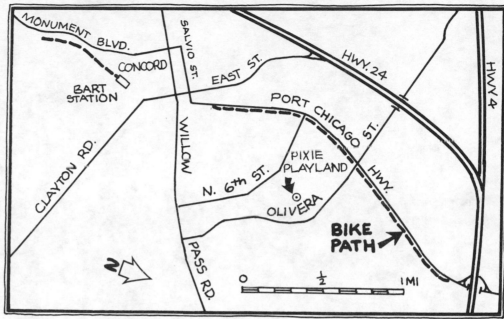

Port Chicago Highway

After the ride, the children might enjoy an outing at Pixie Playland. Located at 2740 East Olivera Road in Willow Pass Park, this amusement park has a merry-go-round, ferris wheel, boat ride, miniature train, and several other rides at a small cost. It is open daily during summer 11–6, the rest of the year on weekends and holidays 11–6. Telephone (415) 689-0220.

The John Muir National Historic Site is a handsome mansion built by the famous environmentalist in 1882. The house is furnished as it was when he lived here, and guides lead interpretive tours through it. Located at 4202 Alhambra Ave., Martinez, it is open daily 8:30–4:30; adults 50 cents, children free. Telephone (415) 228-8860.

A drive through the town of Port Costa on Carquinez Strait is an interesting experience. In the last century, this was a major grain shipping port; today it is a sleepy artist's colony. The kids might enjoy stopping at the Doll Museum at 33 Canyon Lake Drive. Here they can view a collection of 2000 dolls from many historical periods. The museum is open Tuesday through Sunday 10–7; adults $1, children twelve and under 25 cents. Telephone (415) 787-2820.

The Benicia Capitol State Park commemorates the capital of California from 1853 to 1854. The capitol building has been restored and furnished as it was in those days. Located at 1st and G streets in Benicia, it is open daily 10–5; admission 50 cents. Telephone (707) 745-3385.

3   Marin County

Marin County is by far the best-organized county in the Bay Area for providing helpful information to the bicyclist. The Parks and Recreation Department distributes an excellent multicolored map which clearly shows all bike routes in the county; it includes both on-street routes and off-road paths. The map may be obtained free at most bike shops or by mailing a request for "Marin County Bikeways" to Marin County Parks and Recreation Department; County and Civic Center, Room 335; San Rafael, CA 94903; telephone (415) 499-6387.

Although this map is all you need for finding your way around, additional information is available. Marin County Parks and Recreation also publishes a pamphlet called "Guide to Marin County Parks" which provides a brief description of all the county's national, state, county, city, and special district parks; 50 cents. The Golden Gate National Recreation Area publishes a free map and brochure on their facilities in Marin and San Francisco. Write to Superintendent, GGNRA; Fort Mason; San Francisco, CA 94123; telephone (415) 556-0560.

This chapter includes descriptions of six bicycle paths in Marin County. They are:

1. Angel Island: A moderate to difficult, forested loop around the island featuring spectacular views

2. Corte Madera Creek: An easy ride through the fine residential sections of Larkspur, Kentfield, and Ross

3. Redwood Highway: A difficult ride in the rural area alongside Highway 101 north of Marinwood

4. Sausalito Bikeway: An easy path past the houseboats on Richardson Bay

5. Stafford Lake: A moderate path in the rural/residential area west of Novato

6. Tiburon Bikeway: An easy path in the linear park alongside Richardson Bay

Besides these six paths, there are a number of shorter paved paths in Marin County. In Mill Valley, there are paved sections along Camino Alto from Miller to Blithedale and from Camino Alto and Sycamore east to

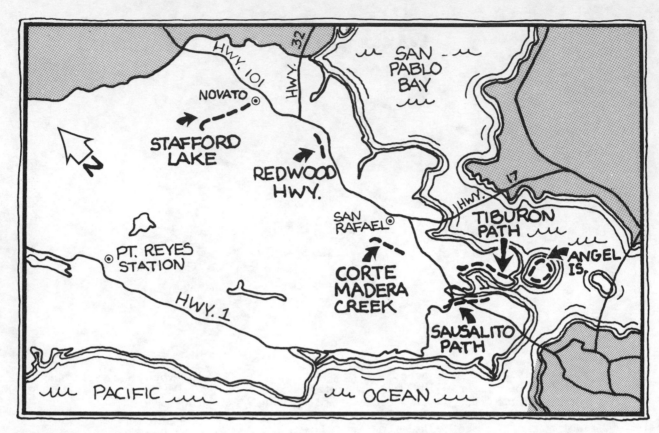

Roque Moraes Drive. In Corte Madera, there is a short path alongside Highway 101 from Lomita Drive to Hawthorne Drive. There are paved paths extending about 0.5 mile in each direction along Sir Francis Drake Boulevard from the Larkspur Ferry Terminal. San Rafael has a short path alongside Highway 101 from the north end of Lincoln Avenue over Los Ranchitos Road to Merrydale Road. In Ignacio, there is a brand-new CALTRANS path along the Northwest Pacific tracks from Hamilton Drive to the Black Point cutoff.

And in Novato, there is a 1 mile path alongside South Novato Boulevard from Sunset Parkway to Lauren Avenue.

There are also a number of very hilly unpaved paths used by bicyclists. These include the "crookedest railroad in the world"—the old railroad grade up Mount Tam starting from West Blithedale Avenue in Mill Valley. Another popular route is around Phoenix Lake from the end of Lagunitas Road in Ross. Finally, the Bear Valley and Coast trails in Point Reyes National Seashore are popular bike routes.

Angel Island

Distance: 5 mile loop

Grade level: Moderate to difficult, with one difficult hill

Path condition: Mostly paved; wide, smooth, well maintained; a few short sections of hard-packed dirt

Topography: Shady; great views of water, hills, forest

Usage: Light to medium traveled

This is a bicycle ride with everything. You get incredible views, beautiful picnic spots, secluded beaches, a relaxing boat ride, and a chance to explore historical remains, as well as an invigorating, hilly bike ride. The trip to Angel Island is normally a full day's outing, so I haven't included any after-the-ride attractions. If you would like some additional activity, look in the sections of this chapter on Tiburon and Sausalito and the sections in Chapter 4 on Golden Gate Bridge and Golden Gate Promenade for suggestions.

Unless you own your own boat, you will begin this trip with a ferry ride. The Angel Island State Park Ferry has small boats operating approximately once an hour from Main Street in Tiburon. Hours are 10–6 daily during the summer and 10–4 on weekends and holidays during the winter. Round-trip fares are adults $2.50, children up to eleven $1.25, bicycles an additional 50 cents each. Telephone (415) 435-2131.

Harbor Carriers operate ferries daily during the summer and on weekends and holidays during the winter, using larger sight-seeing boats with snack and beverage service. These boats connect Pier 43½ at Fisherman's Wharf, San Francisco, with Angel Island and Tiburon. The round-trip fare from San Francisco to Angel Island is $4.50 for adults, $2.50 for children up to eleven. There is no additional charge for bicycles, but plan to arrive at the terminal one hour early as only the first twenty-five bikes are allowed on the boat. Harbor

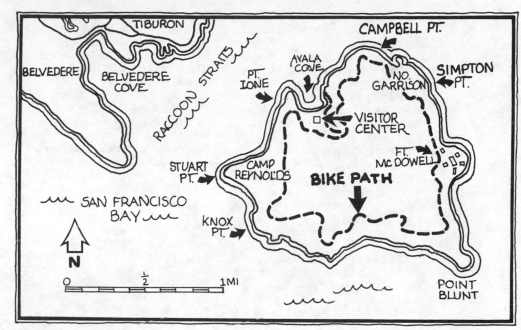

Angel Island

Carriers also operates one ferry boat on summer weekends from Berkeley. Telephone (415) 546-2815 for schedules and more information.

Angel Island was discovered in 1775 by Don Juan Manuel Ayala, captain of the *San Carlos*. Ayala anchored in what is now known as Ayala Cove, the same place where your ferryboat will dock. He used the island, which he named Isla Nuestra Senora de Los Angeles, as a base for his explorations of San Francisco Bay.

The island was granted to Antonio Mario Osio in 1838. Osio brought a herd of cattle over and used the island as grazing land. After the American conquest of California, Osio and the U.S. Army took their conflicting claims to the U.S. Supreme Court. The court found for the army, and the

island has been U.S. or California government property ever since.

Angel Island was used as a prison for rebellious Indians during the early days of California. Later it became infamous as a ground for illegal duels. Around the turn of the century, the island became an immigration detention center, the Ellis Island of the West. Angel Island has also been used as a staging area for soldiers during three wars, a kitchen garden for Alcatraz, and the site of a Nike missile base. Today, except for two small areas at Point Blunt and North Garrison, the entire island is a state park.

All ferry boats dock at Ayala Cove at the north end of the island. Most facilities are in this area, including water, restrooms, picnic tables, grills, a snack bar, and rental bicycles in the summer. The large lawn is very popular with picnickers and is, by far, the most crowded part of the island. Nearby is the visitor center, located in a former quarantine station. The center has a small exhibit room describing the history, flora, and fauna of Angel Island.

Before starting on the ride, check the time and ferry schedule carefully. A loop around the island will take the average family about three hours. This assumes you will want to stop off at various places to rest and explore. So make sure that you will be on time to make the last ferry of the day.

Starting on your bicycle ride, you take the path upward from the visitor center. This is an extremely steep grade rising 100 feet in just over a tenth of a mile. Don't feel ashamed to walk your bike through the cool eucalyptus forest; this is the steepest part of the ride. You soon reach the end of this access road in a T junction. Turn to the right and head west on the perimeter road that circles the island.

You are now on a gentle upslope in a forest of oak, madrone, pine, and cypress. As you come to the crest at Point Ione, you can look back down to Ayala Cove and across the water to Tiburon. Now the path levels out and turns south, giving you a splendid view of Sausalito and Mount Tamalpais. On your right is Camp Reynolds, an old army base with a number of buildings still standing. The schoolhouse and mule barns have been restored, and some of the other buildings are in the process of restoration.

Continuing past an old quarry, you come to the remains of Battery Ledyard. This is a shore battery built in 1900 to command the Golden Gate. The view of the gate from here is spectacular. At this point, a dirt road trails downhill to Perles Beach. If you like, walk on down this road and enjoy a beautiful secluded beach (for sunbathing only; swimming is extremely hazardous). Otherwise rest for a while before you proceed to bike across the southern end of the island.

On the southern end, you have a moderately steep climb up to 300 feet above sea level, with views of San Francisco and Alcatraz. Your climb is rewarded by a very steep downgrade toward Point Blunt Lighthouse. On the descent, you pass a former Nike missile site. I have always been going so fast here that I can't tell you much about the site.

You are now on the east side of the island descending toward Fort McDowell, the largest deserted army base on Angel Island. The old hospital, barracks, and port facilities can be explored. On our last trip, the kids discovered that this deserted army base has the best echoes in the world.

After Fort McDowell, the road climbs steeply to North Garrison, site of the immigration station and now off-limits. Then the path continues across the north end in a series of rolling ups and downs until you come back to the T junction. Now you will enjoy the steep downgrade to Ayala Cove and the ferry slip. If you are taking the last ferry of the day home, you will probably see the Angel Island deer come timidly out of the forest to finish the remains of picnic lunches as your boat leaves the dock.

Corte Madera Creek

Distance: 5.2 miles from William Street to Ross Common and return

Grade level: Easy

Path condition: Paved; wide, smooth

Topography: Mostly shaded; homes, parks, schools

Usage: Light to medium traveled

The Corte Madera Creek path goes through a long-established fine residential section of central Marin County. The beautiful rustic homes here offer a fine contrast to the usual California modern architecture.

To get there, take Tamalpais Drive west from Highway 101. Turn right on Magnolia Avenue, right again on William Street, and park on William, two blocks east of Magnolia in Larkspur. The path goes off to the north along the old railroad right-of-way. The North Pacific Coast Railroad and its successor, the Northwest Pacific, operated passenger trains between 1875 and 1941. Today the tracks have been removed, and the path goes through a forest of redwood and acacia, passing by wild boysenberries, and fine homes.

In two blocks, you pass the tiny old Larkspur train station, now boarded up, with the station sign painted over.

Then you emerge at a shopping mall near downtown Larkspur. Work your way through the parking lot, which is the site of an old sawmill dating from 1847. Then walk across Doherty Avenue and follow the good sidewalk path along Magnolia Avenue.

The path soon curves away from the roadside. On your right is a large open field and a view of hills and tower apartments. On your left, across Magnolia, are some fine old Victorians. You will pass the site of Escalle's, an estate, winery, and inn which was established in 1881. The present owners have restored the picturesque redbrick buildings, but they are not open to the public.

At Bon Air Road, you come to a supermarket and then turn right onto the paved sidewalk. Cross the bridge over the wide, gently flowing Corte Madera Creek. Just north of the creek and just south of Marin General Hospital, you will come to a stoplight. Cross Bon Air here, go past the barrier, and start bicycling to the west alongside the north bank of the creek.

The path follows close to the creek. On your right is a wide marshy area; to your left, you have a good view of the foothills and Mount Tamalpais. There is a par course along this section of the path. So expect a lot of company—joggers, walkers, and bird-watchers.

In half a mile, the creek narrows and then follows a concrete channel. This is a flood control channel built by the Army Corps of Engineers to prevent the floods which used to occur most winters. You are now in Kentfield; across the creek is the

College of Marin stadium and Adeline Kent School. The path crosses the creek on a wooden bridge, passes by the school playing fields, and then comes to College Avenue.

After crossing College, you enter the campus of the College of Marin. This two-year community college was founded in 1926. It is now bursting at the seams, as witnessed by the many temporary buildings interspersed with the older brick and concrete structures. At one of the temporaries, the path vanishes for a short distance. Cut through the parking lot of this building; the path resumes at the edge of the campus.

You soon pass Kentfield Hospital and enter the town of Ross. As you go by some older homes, the path is bordered by eucalyptuses, redwoods, and

acacias. Finally, the path ends at the Ross Post Office, built on the site of the old railroad station. There is no mail delivery in Ross; residents pick up their mail at the post office.

Before returning to Larkspur, spend some time enjoying the English village atmosphere. Across Ross Common is the Ross School, which has a good playground. Further west, just across Lagunitas Avenue, is the town hall, marked by a Bufano bear sculpture. And to the north, at the corner of Lagunitas and Sir Francis Drake Boulevard, is the Marin Art and Garden Center. This 10 acre site has shops, gardens, outdoor theaters, an art gallery, and a tea room. The center

Corte Madera Creek

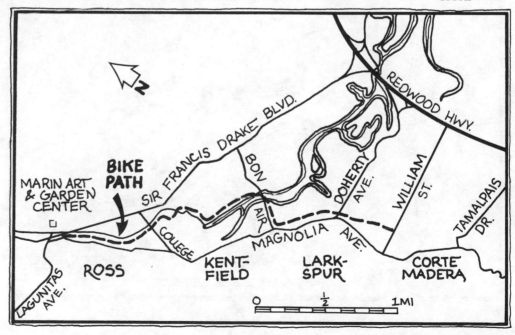

is open daily 9–5; free. Telephone (415) 454-5597.

Nearby San Rafael offers several possibilities for an after-the-ride outing. The Mission San Rafael replica at 5th and A streets has a chapel and museum; open Monday through Saturday 11–4, Sunday 10–4. The Louise A. Boyd Museum of Science has Indian artifacts and wild-life displays, and has a number of injured animals in cages. The museum staff cares for them until they are well enough to survive on their own, at which time they are set free. It is located at 76 Albert Park Lane; telephone (415) 454-6961. Open Tuesday through Saturday 10–4.

Redwood Highway

Distance: 2.5 miles from Miller Creek Road and Marinwood Avenue to Alameda del Prado and return

Grade level: Difficult

Path condition: Paved; wide, smooth, very well maintained

Topography: Open; freeway, meadows, pasturelands

Usage: Very lightly traveled

This path will not be everyone's cup of tea. It is short but strenuous. It is also very close to the freeway and pretty noisy. Nevertheless, it does offer a brisk ride through the beautiful and still lightly developed hills of north-central Marin.

To get there, take the Marinwood exit west from Highway 101 onto Miller Creek Road. Take the first right onto Marinwood Avenue and park as close to the corner as you can. The path begins at the northeast corner of Marinwood and Miller Creek.

The path is built and maintained by CALTRANS. It is very well landscaped; you pass iceplant, pyracantha, pittisporum, and other plantings. The first part of the path is fairly level as you sweep around the curve alongside the freeway offramp.

Once you approach the freeway proper, the path comes quite close to the roadside. But you are screened by a chain link fence, which, together with the bushes, eliminates much of the traffic noise. Now the path begins to climb steeply, ascending 160 feet in 0.4 mile. On your right across the freeway, Pacheco Hill dominates the surroundings; on your left are the grass-covered rolling hills of the Big Rock Ridge. Nearby are attractive two-story homes guarded by a grove of tall eucalyptus trees.

After reaching the crest, the path levels out for a short distance and then descends steeply. At the time of writing, this area was still undeveloped pasture land, but the first signs of construction were beginning to appear. At the bottom of the hill, the path levels out again. You now parallel a small creek bordered by some live oaks in a meadow. Then the path cuts away from the freeway to end at the Alameda del Prado exit.

The area surrounding the end of the path is a part of the Pacheco Valle residential development. So far, most

Redwood Highway

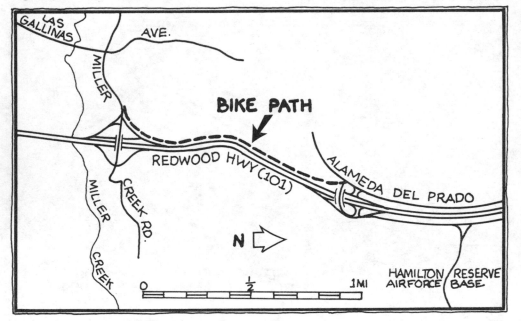

of the development consists of homes and condominiums in the hills far away from the freeway. Rest here for a while before returning. Your trip back will be a little easier, but you still have to climb 90 feet before the long exhilarating downhill run to your car.

Marinwood is not far from the Marin County Civic Center. This spectacular complex designed by Frank Lloyd Wright, with its sky-blue roof, arches, domes, and spires, includes county government buildings and a large auditorium used for theaters and concerts. The nearby fairgrounds and lagoon are part of the county park system. Fishing is permitted from the shore of the lagoon. The Civic Center is open from 7:00 A.M. to 10:00 P.M. on weekdays, and 10:00 A.M. to TO 5:00 P.M. on weekends.

Guide Dogs for the Blind is located at 350 Los Ranchitos Road in north San Rafael. This is a training school for seeing-eye dogs and their masters. Visitors are welcomed Monday through Friday 2–4 and at least one Saturday each month. Telephone (415) 479-4000.

China Camp, on San Pedro Peninsula, was a fishing camp inhabited by Chinese workers who had been employed on the railroads. The camp was closed in 1910; now it is an undeveloped state park with picnic grounds, fishing, hiking, a store, and some deserted buildings from the camp. Rowboats are available for rent if you can locate the proprietor. To be on the safe side, telephone the ranger beforehand at (415) 924-9711 or (415) 456-0766 for more information.

Sausalito Bikeway

Distance: 3.8 miles from Shoreline Highway and Tennessee Avenue to Bridgeway and Wateree Street and return

Grade level: Easy

Path condition: Paved; rough, very narrow

Topography: Open; marshes, bayside, houseboats

Usage: Heavily traveled

This level path on the north edge of Sausalito is not one of my favorites. It is very popular and crowded; in fact, in places it is so narrow that two bikes have to be very careful in passing.

Still, it offers a good variety of interesting and pleasant scenery. If you live nearby, you should try it out.

Parking is a problem for this path. I suggest starting at the north end by taking Shoreline Highway (Hwy. 1) west from Highway 101. Then as soon as you pass the intersection of Tennessee Avenue, park in the lot of one of the many roadside businesses on the right. If you come to the stoplight at Tam Junction, you have gone a block too far. Walk your bikes back along the highway shoulder to the wooden bridge just north of Tennessee Avenue and start bicycling across the bridge.

After crossing the bridge, the path leaves the road, passes a motel, and cuts through a marshy area. The path soon joins the old Northwest Pacific railroad track and then parallels Richardson Bay. You pass a

Sausalito Bikeway

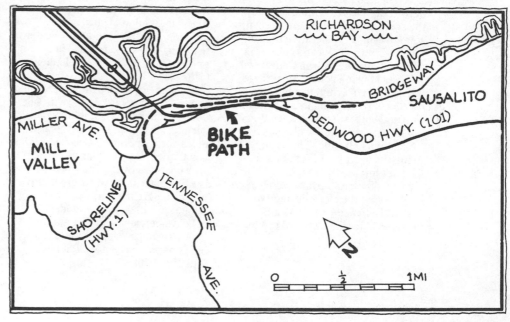

CALTRANS maintenance yard and then go underneath the Richardson Bay Bridge.

On the east side of the bridge is the Marin County Heliport, which provided helicopter service to San Francisco Airport until 1976. The facility is still used for helicopter charter service; there are proposals to resume scheduled service. Next the path passes the mudflats. This section is particularly narrow, so be extra careful when meeting oncoming bicyclists.

At the freeway ramp where Bridgeway merges with the Redwood Highway are the famous Sausalito houseboats. Some of these are very attractive, others are in sad shape, but they are all picturesque. Over the last twenty years, county officials armed with eviction and condemnation notices have tried to get rid of the more decrepit ones, but the occupants have resisted stubbornly. Lately, an agreement has been reached whereby the small houseboaters are to set up a self-governing cooperative to maintain their own docks and collect rents; on the other side, Marin County will relax its housing codes. So perhaps the county government and houseboat dwellers are entering into a state of peaceful coexistence.

The path now follows Bridgeway for about a half-mile. This is an industrial section of north Sausalito. On your left are the remains of Marinship, a 365 acre shipyard which operated around the clock during World War II. Between June 1942 and October 1945, the shipyard produced ninety-three ships and employed over 17,000 workers. As you come to Wateree Street, the path ends; it is time to turn back to your car.

About a half-mile past the south end of the bike path at Bridgeway and Spring Street is the San Francisco Bay Model. This is a scale model which simulates the tidal action, currents, and mixing of salt and fresh water in the Bay. The model is operated by the U.S. Army Corps of Engineers; it is open to the public free of charge Monday through Friday 9–4, and on the first and third Saturdays of each month 9–4; closed holidays. Telephone (415) 332-3870.

Muir Woods National Monument contains some magnificent coast redwoods, viewed from a self-guiding nature trail. Open daily 8:00 A.M. to sunset; adults 50 cents, children free. Telephone (415) 388-2595.

Mount Tamalpais State Park has fantastic views of the whole Bay Area, great hiking trails, campgrounds, and the Mountain Theater, featuring plays and musical programs. Open daily; free. Telephone (415) 388-2070.

Along the coast are Muir Beach and Stinson Beach State Parks, with tidepools, picnicking, swimming (cold!), surfing, hiking, and fishing. Three miles north of Stinson Beach is Audubon Canyon Ranch. This bird nesting area operated by the Audubon Society is a fine place to view the great blue heron and great egret. Open to the public only 10–4 on weekends and holidays between March 1 and July 4; open to groups by appointment; free, but donations accepted. Telephone (415) 383-1644.

Stafford Lake

Distance: 6.4 miles from Sierra Vista Avenue and Novato Boulevard to Stafford Lake and return

Grade level: Moderate

Path condition: Paved; wide, smooth, potholes in a few places

Topography: Mostly shaded; homes, pastures, parks

Usage: Lightly traveled

This is a fairly long, gentle bike ride through a variety of pleasant environments. You start in a fine residential area, go through a rural area, and wind up in a county park.

To get there, take Novato Boulevard west from the center of Novato. Sierra Vista Avenue is one block west of a large shopping center. Turn left onto Sierra Vista and park as close to the corner as possible. Those desiring a shorter ride could start from Miwok Park or San Marin Drive, but I will describe the path as though you were making the entire trip.

The path is on the south side of Novato Boulevard and fairly close to the road. You start up a long, gentle grade of about a half-mile, and then the path levels out. The path is well landscaped and shaded, passing close to a variety of attractive suburban homes. The path is wide and smooth but has some rocks and pebbles on it, so be careful.

At Eucalyptus Avenue, you cross Novato Boulevard at a crosswalk. The path then follows the north side of the Boulevard across Novato Creek and past Miwok Park. This linear park, which parallels the creek for about a half-mile, has a shady, paved bike path, picnic tables, grassy playing fields, and a very nice playground under the oaks. It also contains the Marin Miwok Museum (more about that later).

Continuing west from Miwok Park, the path is alternately narrow and wide. You pass more homes in a pretty valley with grass-covered hillsides on both sides. There are still a few orchards left in this section. You soon come to the corner of San Marin Drive.

There are paved bike trails on both sides of Novato-Hicks Valley Road (Novato Boulevard changes its name at this intersection) for a short distance from San Marin Drive. On the north side is the attractive redwood-faced San Marin High School. At a PG&E station, the path on the north side ends, and you must cross back to the south side.

You now pass some horse pastures, corrals, and fields colorful with wildflowers in the spring. This part of the path has very little shade and is a slow but steady upgrade. After crossing a small creek, the path cuts away from the roadside and passes through a cool oak forest. Look for the rickety wooden bridge on your left with a turnstile to discourage bicycle riders. The bridge leads to a fishing hole on Novato Creek and to some hiking trails through Marin Water District lands.

The path approaches the road again at the entrance to Indian Valley Golf Course. At this point, you come to the one fairly steep portion of the trail, a 60 foot climb in about 0.1 mile. From the crest, you have a view of Novato Creek Dam and Stafford Lake.

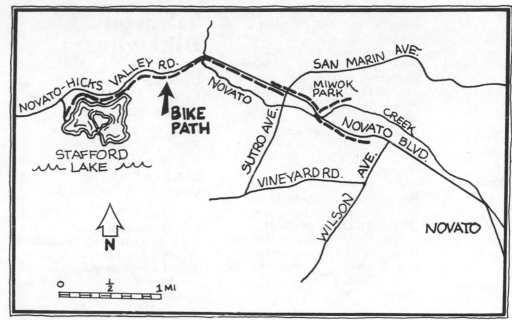

Stafford Lake

The portion of the path along the lakeside has cracked in several places and is encroached on by parked cars. However, you soon enter the boundaries of the county park, and the path immediately leaves the roadside and improves considerably, rolling up and down to the lakeside.

Stafford Lake County Park offers picnicking, hiking, fishing, and ballplaying. The lake is in a beautiful bowl of green hills overlooked by grazing cattle. There is an admission charge of $1 per car, but bicyclists get in for free. This is a good place to relax and eat your lunch before returning down the path to your car.

The Marin Miwok Museum has displays of Indian artifacts, geologic specimens, and scientific and historical collections. It is located in Miwok City Park on Novato Boulevard. Open Tuesdays through Saturdays 10–4, Sunday 12–4, closed most holidays. A donation of 50 cents for adults and 25 cents for children is suggested. Telephone (415) 897-4064.

A few miles west of Stafford Lake in Hicks Valley is The Cheese Factory, 7500 Red Hill Road. Formerly called the Marin French Cheese Company, this business has operated continuously since 1865. It offers a factory tour and cheese tasting. Open daily 10–4; telephone (707) 762-6001. Also in Hicks Valley are several one-room schoolhouses which are still in use. One of them, the Union District School, is located on Red Hill Road about 2 miles north of The Cheese Factory.

Continuing to the west for 16 more miles, you will reach Point Reyes National Seashore. This area has a number of fine hiking trails, a visitor center, a lighthouse open to visitors, a reconstructed Indian village, and an earthquake trail. Parking is free, and there is also a free shuttlebus to the beach during the summer. The Bear Creek and Coast trails are popular with bicyclists even though they are unpaved and rather hilly. Telephone (415) 663-1092.

Three miles east of Petaluma is the Petaluma Adobe State Historical Monument. This is a restoration of the massive adobe home built by General Mariano Vallejo in 1836. Open daily 10–5, closed most holidays; admission is 50 cents for adults, free for children. Telephone (707) 762-4871.

Tiburon Bikeway

Distance: 4.8 miles from Blackie's Pasture to Beach Road and return

Grade level: Easy

Path condition: Paved; wide, smooth, well maintained

Topography: Partly shaded, partly open; park, homes, bay

Usage: Heavily traveled

The Tiburon bikeway offers a scenic, easy ride along the sunny side of Richardson Bay. This ride can be combined with a ferry ride, and, if desired, a more strenuous ride around Angel Island.

Begin by parking in the very large dirt lot at the corner of Tiburon Boulevard and Greenwood Beach Road. This is the pasture where a sway-backed horse named Blackie grazed for twenty-five years until his death in 1966 at the age of forty. Blackie is buried in the pasture, which is named for him; a white picket fence marks his grave.

The bike path takes off from the parking area. Like so many of the Bay Area bike paths, it is built on an old railroad right-of-way. The San Francisco and North Pacific Railroad and its successor, the Northwest Pacific, provided freight and passenger service from San Rafael to Tiburon between 1884 and 1967. The tracks have been removed, and the smooth, wide path was installed in 1971.

At the start of the path is a well-maintained par course. You are now in Richardson Bay Park, a linear park operated by the city of Tiburon. The park features a large grassy area next to the bay, ideal for picnicking. This part of the path is very popular and crowded. You should probably stop to enjoy the superb views of Sausalito and San Francisco.

After leaving the park, the path approaches closer to Tiburon Boulevard. The intervening hills and trees—mostly redwood and eucalyptus—effectively shield you from traffic noise. Soon you come to San Rafael Avenue, the western approach road to Belvedere. A curb barrier forces you to dismount and walk your bike across the street.

The remainder of the path is sandwiched between Tiburon Boulevard and a residential section fronting on

Tiburon Bikeway

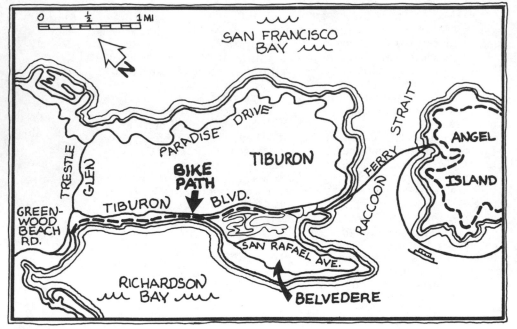

Belvedere Lagoon. Again, the land-scaping shields you from traffic noise. At Cove Road, you enter the business section of Tiburon. The path continues for one more block, finally ending at Beach Road.

From here, it is a short walk to Main Street, downtown Tiburon. This is an interesting tourist center, packed with restaurants, bars, and shops. The false-fronted buildings recall the architecture of Tiburon when it was a bustling railroad town during the last century. Along Main Street is the dock for the Angel Island and San Francisco ferries. The ferry ride is described in the section on Angel Island.

Old St. Hilary's Historic Preserve is a half-mile beyond downtown Tiburon at the tip of the peninsula. The preserve contains a picturesque church, a botanical garden, a history and a botany museum, and a rare collection of wildflowers. The preserve is open daily during daylight hours, the museum on Sundays and Wednesdays from 1–4. Telephone (415) 435-1853.

The Tiburon Uplands Nature Preserve on the north side of the peninsula has some beautiful, hilly hiking paths. The nearby Paradise Beach County Park has a fishing pier, swimming beach, and picnic area. The park is open daily from 7:00 A.M. to sunset; parking is $1 per car on weekdays and $2 on weekends. Telephone (415) 499-6387.

The Richardson Bay Wildlife Sanctuary is at 376 Greenwood Beach Road, near Blackie's Pasture. This is a bird refuge with a nature trail; open Wednesday through Sunday 9–5. The headquarters for the sanctuary is a restored Victorian home built in 1876. The home is open Saturday and Sunday 1–4; adults $1, children 50 cents, Audubon Society members free. Telephone (415) 388-2524.

4 San Francisco County

The California Department of Transportation (CALTRANS) publishes a San Francisco Bay Touring Guide. This includes a map of bicycle routes in San Francisco, commuter bike routes in the other Bay Area counties, transbay crossing information, and other information of interest to bicycle commuters. It can be obtained by writing to Department of Transportation; P.O. Box 3366, Rincon Annex; San Francisco, CA 94119; telephone (415) 557-1840.

The Golden Gate National Recreation Area publishes a free map and brochure on their facilities in Marin County and San Francisco. Write to Superintendent, GGNRA; Fort Mason; San Francisco, CA 94123; telephone (415) 556-0560.

This chapter includes descriptions of five bicycle paths in San Francisco County. They are:

1. Golden Gate Bridge: A moderate path high above the entrance to San Francisco Bay

2. Golden Gate Park: A moderate path through this beautiful, forested city park

3. Golden Gate Promenade: An easy ride through the Presidio and San Francisco's northern waterfront

4. Lake Merced: An easy to moderate loop around a scenic lake in the southwest corner of the city

5. Sunset Bikeway: A moderate path through a fine residential section along Sunset Boulevard

Golden Gate Bridge

Distance: 3.8 miles from San Francisco View Point to Marin Vista Point and return

Grade level: Moderate

Path condition: Concrete sidewalk; wide, smooth

Topography: Open; bridge and water

Usage: Heavily traveled

This is one of the most dramatic bicycle rides you will ever make. You go across the beautiful and world-famous bridge, while far below ships from faraway ports are continually entering and leaving the harbor. You will enjoy spectacular views of the hills of Marin County; the sparkling skyline of San Francisco; the ocean, bay, and islands. Bring warm clothes; this can be a very cold ride even on a hot summer day.

To get there from San Francisco, take the Golden Gate Bridge approach (Highway 101, Doyle Drive) toward the bridge. Just before the toll plaza, note the sign reading "View Area–Presidio–GGNRA." Turn right here and enter the view area; turn left at the stop sign and park in the lot.

San Francisco County

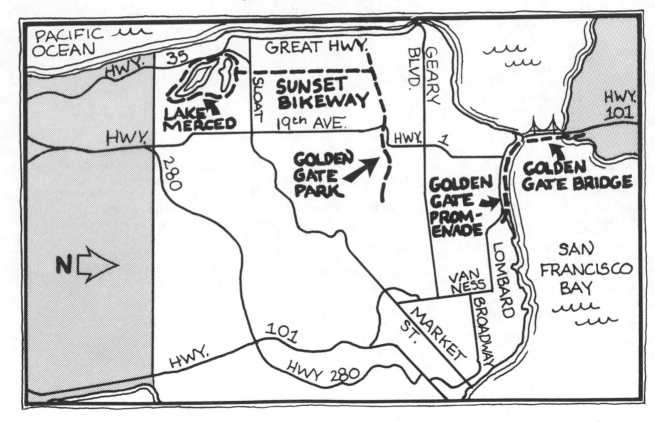

From Marin County, if you plan to go into San Francisco after the ride, cross the bridge by car. Get into the rightmost lane at the toll plaza, pay the $1.25 toll, and take an immediate right turn at the sign reading "25th Avenue." Keep bearing right, go under the roadway, and enter the view area.

If you are coming from Marin and don't wish to pay the toll, simply turn off the highway just before crossing the bridge at the sign reading "Golden Gate National Recreation Area." Then park in the large lot next to the highway and follow the ride in a north-to-south direction.

The San Francisco View Area is beautifully landscaped; note particularly the large clumps of grape hyacinth. The area is always crowded with tourists admiring the views, taking pictures, and examining the statue of Joseph B. Strauss, chief engineer during construction of the bridge. There is a gravel path leading down to Fort Point. The path is built in a series of switchbacks so that, even though it descends 175 feet, it is not too steep. You can bicycle down if you are reasonably careful, but you won't enjoy pushing your bike back up the path!

To start the ride across the bridge, bicycle up the roadway toward the circular building—headquarters for the Golden Gate Transit District. After reaching the sidewalk, you will see a sign directing bicyclists to take the east sidewalk (the one you are

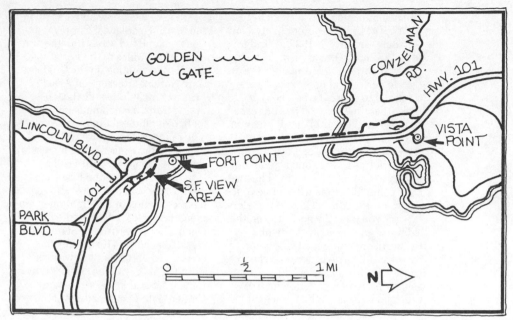

Golden Gate Bridge

already on) on weekdays and the west sidewalk on weekends. Since I have always taken this ride on a Saturday or Sunday, I will describe the trip that way. Signs will direct you to an asphalt path which leads down under the bridge and then back up to the sidewalk on the west (ocean) side.

From the San Francisco approach abutment to mid-span, the elevation increases by 80 feet. While the climb is very gradual, you may find it tiring after a while, especially if there is a strong wind. If so, stop and enjoy the scenery. Warn your group to be careful while bicycling, especially on windy days. Though there are barriers on both the water and the road sides, there is a high curb on the inside of the sidewalk. Daydreaming

can result in an unpleasant, although not catastrophic, accident.

Signs direct the bicyclist to get off and walk his bike around the towers. This is a good rule, although many bicyclists ignore it. Note how massive the towers are—they extend 746 feet above the water, about the height of a sixty-five-story building.

Before the bridge was built, Marin County travelers relied on ferryboats. In 1928, the state formed the Golden Gate Bridge, Highway, and Transit District, and construction on the bridge began in 1933. Even though the work was plagued by high winds, fog, several deaths, and a ship which crashed into and destroyed an access trestle, the bridge was completed on schedule on May 27, 1937. A bridge toll of 25 cents per car in each direction was sufficient revenue for the district to perform maintenance operations and to retire the bonds by 1971. Since that time, the toll has increased to $1.25 (in the southbound direction only), and the district has gone into the transit business, operating an excellent bus system and a good, but money losing, ferry system. Thus we have come full circle with ferries once again serving Marin County travelers.

After you pass the north tower, the sidewalk goes gradually downhill to the north anchorage. At this point, the bicyclist must travel across a concrete causeway to the near hillside. An asphalt path then goes downhill to Conzelman Road. When you get to the road, turn left to go steeply uphill for a climb of about 70 feet; traffic is very light on this road. Soon you approach the large parking lot in which our friends from Marin County who didn't wish to pay the toll parked.

From the parking lot, walk your bikes on the pedestrian walkway down and under the bridge and then up a flight of stairs to the Vista Point parking area. Here you will find an interpretive kiosk, a slice of a giant redwood tree washed up at Stinson Beach, restrooms, many tourists, and a spectacular view of San Francisco and the bay. After enjoying the amenities and resting, return to San Francisco by retracing your route.

After the ride, how about a trip to the Marin Headlands? Simply take Conzelman Road west from the bridge for 5 miles to the Fort Cronkhite Ranger Station (in the Golden Gate National Recreation Area). Features include a sandy beach, hiking trails, a small museum, and a lot of old military bunkers to explore. The rangers lead nature walks and tours of a Nike missile site by reservation; telephone (415) 561-7612.

In San Francisco, the Fire Department Museum at 655 Presidio Avenue has a collection of fire-fighting equipment dating from 1850 to the present. Open Thursday through Sunday 1–4; free. Telephone (415) 558-3949.

A trip to Fort Point is always interesting. This Civil War-era fort is more fully described in the section on the Golden Gate Promenade. Another interesting place to visit is the Musee Mecanique at the Cliff House. Here you will find a collection of coin-operated antique mechanical contrivances, including a toothpick carnival, nickelodeons, strength testers, and the like. Open Monday through Friday 11–6, weekends and holidays 10–7; free (but you supply the coins to operate the machines). Telephone (415) 386-1170

Golden Gate Park

Distance: 5.2 miles from 47th Avenue to California Academy of Sciences and return

Grade level: Moderate

Path condition: Paved; western half is narrow; eastern half is on a broad roadway

Topography: Shady, forested park

Usage: Very heavily traveled

There is a paved bicycle path covering the western half of Golden Gate Park, and on Sundays automobile traffic is not allowed on some of the roads in the eastern half. So bicyclists can enjoy a shady, traffic-free ride with ample opportunities to stop and visit the interesting attractions in this enormously varied park.

Prior to 1870, the site was covered by sand dunes with a few rocky areas, marshes, and stands of coast live oak. In that year, the city established Golden Gate Park, and under engineer William Hall and superintendent John McLaren, development began. The park was the site of the 1894 Mid-winter International Exposition, for which the Japanese Tea Garden, de Young Museum, and other facilities were built. Golden Gate Park was a temporary residence for hundreds of homeless San Franciscans after the 1906 earthquake. Since that time, development has continued, until the park has become a world-famous recreation area and a masterpiece of landscape architecture.

Begin by parking at the corner of 47th Avenue and Lincoln Way near the southwest corner of the park. If you can't find a space, try parking along South Drive; if you still have trouble, then park in the paved parking lot in the center of Great Highway at the oceanfront.

The bike path enters the park at 47th Avenue. It is paved, fairly narrow, and well shaded by pine and cypress trees. You climb a reasonably steep hill as soon as you enter the park, then carefully walk your bikes across South Drive. Next, bike up and down another hill, cross Chain of Lakes Drive, and bike past South Lake to the Polo Field.

The Polo Field is a stadium with a few rows of bleachers, used more often for track or football than for polo. Circling the field is a wide paved track about a mile around. Kids and adults enjoy riding or racing their bikes around the track.

From the Polo Field, the path continues alongside a picnic ground, ending at John F. Kennedy Drive opposite Lloyd Lake. Across the lake, notice Portals of the Past, the portico of the A. N. Towne residence, which was erected here in 1909 as a memorial to those whose homes had been destroyed in the earthquake.

If you are taking this ride on a Monday through Saturday, you will have to use the wide sidewalk for the rest of the trip. This sidewalk will get progressively more crowded with walkers, joggers, bicyclists, skateboarders, and roller skaters, so you may have to dismount and walk your

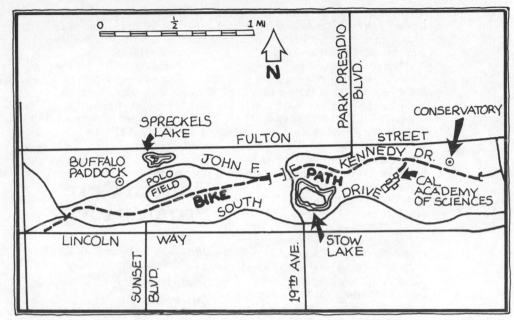

Golden Gate Park

bicycles. On Sundays, cars are not allowed on Kennedy Drive east of Transverse Drive and the connecting streets between 7:00 A.M. and dusk, so you can ride on the wide roadway. Even so, you will find it very crowded and will have to work your way carefully around the skaters and others.

You pass Prayerbook Cross at Rainbow Falls, a memorial to the first English language religious service in California (Drake's Bay, 1579), the entrance road to Stow Lake, and the back of the de Young Museum. Then, at the most crowded part of the park, turn right onto the entrance road to the Music Concourse and the California Academy of Sciences.

The academy is a cluster of excellent physical and natural science

museums. Plan to spend at least several hours visiting them. The complex includes Steinhart Aquarium with its fish roundabout, exhibits of stuffed African and North American animals, the Wattis Hall of Man, an astronomy and space museum, and the Morrison Planetarium. The academy is open daily 10–5 with later summer hours; adults $1, twelve–seventeen years old 50 cents, five–eleven years old 25 cents; planetarium shows cost $1.50 for adults and 50 cents for children under eighteen. Telephone (415) 752-8268 for recorded information.

After leaving the academy, you will probably want to return to your car.

Or you might wish to continue along Kennedy Drive to the Conservatory. This attractive glass-walled structure, modeled after Kew Gardens in London, was originally planned for the San Jose estate of James Lick. After Lick's death in 1876, it was presented by his estate to the city and assembled in Golden Gate Park. The Conservatory maintains a continual showing of permanent and seasonal plants and flowers. Outside is the beautiful and chronologically accurate Floral Clock, a gift of the Watchmakers of Switzerland and the Retail Jewelers of San Francisco. The Conservatory is open daily 8–4:50; free.

There are a number of other interesting places to visit within the park. Children's Playground at South and Kezar drives has a carousel, tiny farm, an old cable car for climbing, a small roller coaster, and a snack bar. Nearby is the Bowling Green, where you can watch the lawn bowlers.

The Japanese Tea Garden has beautiful gardens, pagodas, pools, waterfalls, bridges, and a tea house; open daily 10:30–5; adults 50 cents, six–twelve years old 25 cents, under six free. The Strybing Arboretum has a fine collection of trees, shrubs, and flowers; open Monday through Friday 8–4:30, Saturday, Sunday and holidays 10–5; free. Telephone (415) 661-1316.

The boathouse at Stow Lake rents rowboats, Lo-power, and pedal boats; open Tuesday through Sunday 9–4. Telephone (415) 752-0347.

Other park activities are watching model boat sailing on Spreckels Lake, looking at the elk and bison in the buffalo paddock, fly casting, archery, golf, baseball, and horseshoes. Telephone (415) 558-3706 for additional information.

Golden Gate Promenade

Distance: 3.8 miles from Fort Point to Exploratorium and return

Grade level: Easy

Path condition: Poor—partly paved, partly gravel; varies from very narrow to very wide; disappears at several places

Topography: Open; military buildings, bay, park

Usage: Medium to heavily traveled

I agonized for a long time over whether to include this path in the book. On the one hand, the Golden Gate Promenade is so well known that it would seem peculiar to leave it out. Also, it is an interesting trip with unique views of the Golden Gate and the bridge. And the two attractions at either end of the path are great places to visit. On the other hand, the condition of the path is so terrible that it

detracts from the pleasure and safety of the ride. On balance, I recommend it provided that your group will be extremely careful in riding it.

Be sure to dress warmly for this ride. Begin by getting to the view point area at the San Francisco end of the Golden Gate Bridge. From San Francisco, take Doyle Drive and make a right turn just before the toll plaza at the sign saying "View Area–Presidio– GGNRA." From Marin County, turn right just after the toll plaza at the sign reading "25th Avenue" and keep bearing right under the bridge to the view area. From the view area, take the exit road south to Lincoln Boulevard. Make a left on Lincoln, go down the hill, and make a sharp left at Long Avenue. Long runs into Marine Drive; park on Marine at the seawall near Fort Point.

Before starting, why not visit Fort Point? This three-story brick fort is directly under the bridge. It was built by the U.S. Army during the Civil War, following the design of Fort Sumter. The guns which command the entrance to San Francisco Bay were never fired in battle. The fort is now a museum operated by the National Park Service; it is a fascinating place to explore. Open daily except January 1 and December 25, 10–5; free. Telephone (415) 556-1693.

The first tenth of a mile of the path is simply a stripe on Marine Drive separating bicycles from parked cars and the seawall chain. Since the surf crashes against the seawall (the roadway crumbled disastrously during a storm in 1980), and since the pavement is very slippery, please walk your bikes along this section. Then at the corner where Long leaves Marine, the path becomes ridable.

The path is first a narrow cut between buildings, passing behind the Presidio motor pool and then becoming a dirt trail. It follows close to the water's edge past the Fort Point fishing dock, then ends at the Presidio Coast Guard Station. The station has very attractive red-roofed, white-shingled buildings, and palm trees. It is a life-saving facility which is kept busy rescuing stranded boaters. Bicyclists must ride through the Coast Guard parking lot for a short distance.

After the Coast Guard Station, the path follows a broad, paved, abandoned runway on Crissy Field for 0.7 mile. Then it goes on a paved bike path along a sandy beach for another 0.6 mile. There is a par course along this section, so it is normally pretty crowded. This section, like the whole path, is perfectly flat and treeless and offers a good view of the Golden Gate, the bridge, the islands, and Marin County.

At the point where you leave the Presidio, the path ends at some broad shallow steps. Walk your bike up the steps, past the Municipal Water Treatment Facility. Then cut left at the access road to the St. Francis Yacht Club and cut right at the rings station on the par course. You should now be going away from the water on a little pathway through the Marina Green. Carefully cross Marina Boulevard at the crosswalk and take the sidewalk on the south side of Marina to your right for one block until you come to the Palace of Fine Arts, site of the Exploratorium.

The Exploratorium is one of the most exciting museums anywhere for both children and adults. It is a science museum with many displays in optics, sound, mechanics, electricity, and electronics. All of the exhibits allow hands-on participation. You will find it most difficult to drag all of your group away even after several hours. The Exploratorium is open Wednesday through Friday 1–5, Saturday and Sunday 12–5, Wednesday evening 7–9:30. There is no admission, but donations of $1 per person are encouraged. Telephone (415) 563-3200 for a twenty-four-hour recorded message, or (415) 563-7337 for the administrative office. The Palace of Fine Arts is a beautiful neo-classical structure, all that remains of the 1915 Panama-Pacific World's Fair. It surrounds a small lagoon with ducks and swans, a great place to have a picnic lunch.

The Golden Gate Promenade continues for another 1.3 miles to Fort Mason, but this section is really just a crowded sidewalk on the north side of Marina Boulevard. You may choose to take this path or to head back to Fort Point.

Fort Mason is the headquarters for the Golden Gate National Recreation

Golden Gate Promenade

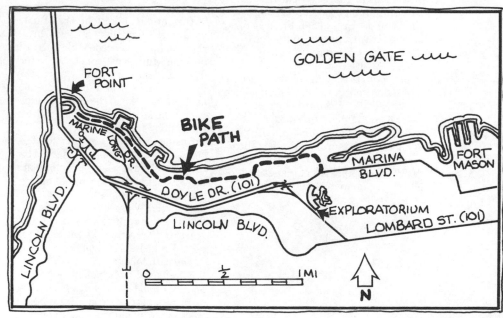

Area. Most weekends there will be a wide variety of cultural, educational, and recreational programs. Telephone (415) 441-5705 to find out the current schedule.

A few blocks further east is the National Maritime Museum, which consists of an indoor museum with nautical exhibits plus the Hyde Street Pier, with four historic ships for self-guided touring. The museum is open daily 10–5; free. Telephone (415) 556-8177. The pier is open daily 10–6 in summer, 10–5 in winter; free. Telephone (415) 556-6435.

Nearby are the tourist areas of Ghirardelli Square, The Cannery, Fisherman's Wharf, and Pier 39. At these areas, you will find such attractions as Ripley's Believe It or Not Museum, two wax museums, Enchanted World of San Francisco, a helicopter ride, harbor tours, the sailing ship *Balclutha,* and many others. All are commercial operations, open daily, with substantial admission charges. The National Park Service leads tours of the former federal penitentiary on Alcatraz Island, leaving from Fisherman's Wharf. These tours require ferryboat reservations well in advance. Cost is $2.50 for adults, $1.25 for ages five–eleven. Telephone Harbor Tours at (415) 546-2805.

Lake Merced

Distance: 5.2 mile loop around the lake

Grade level: Easy to moderate

Path condition: Paved; wide, fairly smooth

Topography: Partly open, partly shady; lake, woods, golf course, homes

Usage: Medium to heavily traveled

This is a pleasant, relatively level loop with a lot of interesting places to stop. You can begin this ride at any of a number of parking lots around the lake; I will describe the ride beginning from the southwest side of the lake.

To get there, take John Daly Boulevard west from Highway 280. Turn right on Lake Merced Boulevard, left on John Muir Drive, and proceed for 0.3 mile along John Muir. Park at the dirt parking lot opposite a concrete bridge that cuts off the southernmost end of the lake. Start biking north on the path by John Muir Drive.

During the last century, Lake Merced was a small lagoon connected to the ocean by a stream. Sometime in the 1890s, the stream was cut off by the development of sand dunes. Today Lake Merced is a freshwater lake fed by a spring; it is used as an emergency reservoir by the San Francisco Water Department.

The path follows close to the road. It is well used by bicyclists, joggers, and walkers. For the most part, it is open, although there are a number of trees in the vicinity, including eucalyptus, cypress, pine, silk, and others.

There is also plentiful ground cover, including wildflowers, ferns, berries, and ice plant.

You soon pass the Pacific Rod and Gun Club, which is open to the public for target shooting. The club has a sign proudly proclaiming that they have had no accidents in fifty years. After climbing a gradual slope to Skyline Boulevard, you pass the San Francisco Police Pistol Range. This range is not open to the public.

Just north of the intersection of Skyline Boulevard and Great Highway, Harding Road enters the park. Cross Harding and turn right on the bike path on the north side of the road. This leads you to the narrow isthmus cutting the lake in two, where you will find a number of picnic tables in a very well-maintained lawn. There are two small wooden platforms on the lakeshore from which you can feed the ducks. Across the road is the boathouse, which includes a coffee shop, snack bar, and cocktail lounge. You can rent rowboats here or take sailing lessons; open daily 9:00 A.M. to dusk. Telephone (415) 566-0300.

Return to Skyline Boulevard and continue to the north. Now you come to the start of the Perrier par course. This course is unusual in that it emphasizes a heart check—at each station, the user is encouraged to check his heart beat immediately after exercising.

When you come to the corner of Lake Merced Boulevard, the path curves to the right; you are now going east along Lake Merced. There is a large parking lot at the corner of Lake

Merced and Sunset boulevards. Take a right turn and go to the southwest corner of the lot. Now take the narrow paved footpath (suitable for biking) down the steep hill to the peaceful wooden footbridge. Cross the bridge and go up the steep hill, past the stand of eucalyptus to the Harding Park Municipal Golf Course's clubhouse area. The golf course is public property; there are also restrooms, a restaurant, and a pro shop here. After a short stop, return across the footbridge to Lake Merced Boulevard.

Continuing east, you now have good views of the great TV tower on Mount Sutro, the cross on Mount Davidson, and the range of radio antennas on Mount San Bruno. After a long, gradual descent past Brotherhood Way, you will soon see the concrete bridge again. You can now cheat by biking across the bridge or continue on for the full circuit of the lake.

The south end of the lake is shallow, bordered with tule rushes, and is a popular resting spot for birds. Before you reach the intersection of Lake Merced and John Muir, notice a sign pointing to the site of the Broderick-Terry duel. U.S. Senator David Broderick and California Supreme Court Chief Justice David Terry were both pioneers of 1849 who rose rapidly in California politics. They became aligned with rival factions of the Democratic party in the 1859 elections, rhetoric escalated, and on the morning of September 13, 1859, they met on the field of honor at this spot. Broderick received a mortal wound. With such sobering thoughts mingling with the sounds of shots from the Rod and Gun Club, return on John Muir Drive to your car.

The Lake Merced bike path connects with several other paths. There

is the Sunset Bikeway described in the next section. There is also a good sidewalk path leading east on Brotherhood Way to 19th Avenue, and a path south along Lake Merced Boulevard to Westlake Park in Daly City. Any of these may be used to extend your ride.

After the ride, you might enjoy a trip to the beach. There are several nearby—Ocean Beach and Fort Funston in San Francisco, Thornton State Beach in Daly City. They have sandy beaches and sand dunes; Thornton also has a fishing pier.

You could also visit Sanchez Adobe, a restored Spanish Ranch House in Pacifica. Located on Linda Mar Boulevard; open Tuesday and Sunday only, 1–5; free. Telephone (415) 359-1462.

James V. Fitzgerald Marine Reserve is an outdoor museum in Moss Beach. Rangers lead lectured tours of the beach and tidepools; open daily 8–5. Telephone (415) 728-3584.

Sunset Bikeway

Distance: 5.8 miles from Lake Merced Boulevard to Polo Field and return

Grade level: Moderate

Path condition: Paved; fairly wide, smooth

Topography: Shady; landscaped parkway, homes, schools

Usage: Medium traveled

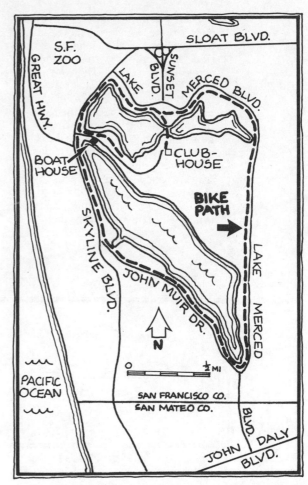

Lake Merced

The Sunset bikeway is a good sidewalk path along a landscaped parkway in the handsome Sunset residential district. The ride may be taken either separately or in combination with the Lake Merced path to the south or the Golden Gate Park path to the north.

There is another possible variation on this route, which you may be able to take so as to make a loop out of the ride. On windy days, when sand drifts across the road, Great Highway is closed to autos from Lincoln Way to Sloat Boulevard. Then you could bike up Great Highway, across the park on the sidewalk path by South Drive, down the Sunset bikeway, and west on the sidewalk path at Sloat. I don't recommend this route; Great Highway is a sandy and uninteresting road. However, if you get a kick out of safely biking down the middle of what is normally a busy highway, then drive to the west end of Sloat to see if the road is closed to autos.

If you aren't planning to try the Great Highway loop route, then park in the large paved lot at the south corner of Sunset and Lake Merced boulevards. Cross Lake Merced and start biking on the asphalt path on the west side of Sunset.

The path starts up a long gentle incline leading to Wawona Street. It then goes steeply downhill for a block to Vicente, and steeply uphill for two blocks to Taraval before leveling out. The path is reasonably wide and usually not too crowded. Sunset Boulevard is well landscaped, with many flowers and cypress, pine, fir, and sycamore trees. A block away on each side are the fine two-story homes of the Sunset district, each one touching its neighbor.

From Rivera to Ortega streets, there is a break in the line of homes on the west. This section includes several schools and the West Sunset Playground. On a clear day, you have a fine view of the ocean and the coastline extending north to Point Reyes.

The path remains level to Lawton, then goes fairly steeply downhill and under Lincoln Way into Golden Gate Park. Cross South Drive and turn right on the sidewalk path. Then look for the path branching off to your left to the Polo Field.

The Polo Field has a wide, paved circumferential track which you will enjoy racing around. After spending some time here, turn around and follow Sunset bikeway back to your car, unless you decide to continue your bike ride by taking the Golden Gate Park path (described in a previous section).

The San Francisco Zoo on Sloat Boulevard is a fun place to visit after your ride. This is a very large municipal zoo with a playground, children's zoo, and several rides. Open daily 10–5, weather permitting; adults $2, under fifteen free when accompanied by an adult; children's zoo is 50 cents per person. Telephone (415) 661-4844.

The Josephine Randall Junior Museum has a collection of small, caged animals, some of which may be held and petted, plus science exhibits and a model train layout. Located at 199 Museum Way; open Tuesday through Saturday, 10–5 during the

Sunset Bikeway

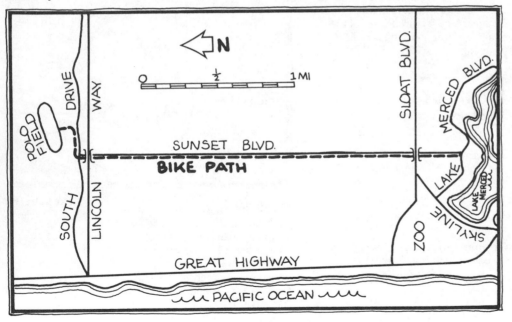

school year, Monday through Friday 10–5 in the summer; free. Telephone (415) 863-1399. To get there, take Lincoln Way east, turn right on Stanyan Street, left on 17th Street, left on Roosevelt Way, and right on Museum Way.

Mission Dolores is one of the oldest and most beautiful of the chain of California missions. Located at 16th and Dolores streets; open daily 9:30–4:30 May through October, daily 10–4 November through April; free but donations accepted. Telephone (415) 431-2544. To get there, take Lincoln Way east, turn right on Stanyan Street, left on 17th Street, and follow 17th to Dolores.

5 San Mateo County

San Mateo County Parks and Recreation Department publishes a map of bike routes in the county plus a map of Coyote Point Park. Both may be obtained free of charge by writing to San Mateo County Parks and Recreation Department; County Office Building; Redwood City, CA 94063; telephone (415) 364-5600.

The cities of San Mateo and Daly City publish free maps of bike routes within their limits. For the first, write to San Mateo City Parks and Recreation Department; City Hall, 330 West 20th Avenue; San Mateo, CA 94403; telephone (415) 574-6730. For the second, write to Daly City Recreation Department; 134 Hillside Boulevard; Daly City, CA 94014; telephone (415) 992-5356.

This chapter includes descriptions of six bicycle paths in San Mateo County. They are:

1. Alpine Road: A moderate forested path in a fine residential section of Portola Valley

2. Bayfront Trail: An easy ride through a bird sanctuary by the bay in Foster City

3. Canada Road: A moderate boulevard with beautiful scenery near Crystal Springs Reservoir, available for bicycling seven days a year

4. Coyote Point Park: A moderate ride through the forested county park on the bay in San Mateo

5. Ralston Cutoff: A difficult, peaceful ride through the hills of upper Belmont

6. Sawyer's Camp Road: A moderate to difficult shady ride through undeveloped water district property west of San Mateo

In addition to these six, there are several shorter paths in the county. In Foster City, there is a paved path circling Central Park and another short path between Anchor Road and Mariner's Island Boulevard. San Bruno

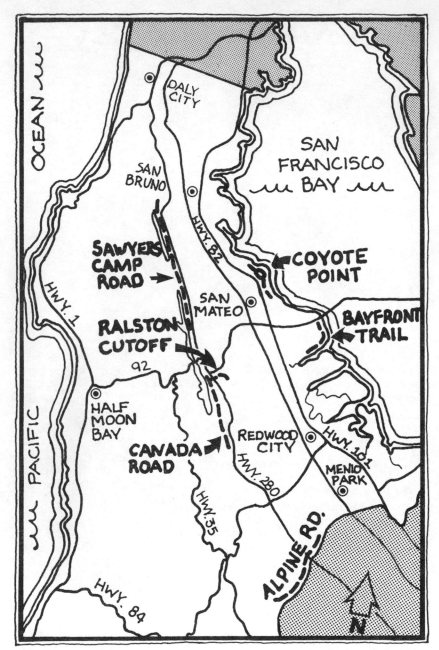

has several short paths radiating from San Bruno City Park. Burlingame has a section of the Bayfront Trail near Airport Boulevard east of Broadway. Daly City has a paved path along Lake Merced Boulevard from Westlake Park to the Lake Merced bicycle path in San Francisco.

Alpine Road

Distance: 8.4 miles from Junipero Serra Boulevard to Portola Road and return

Grade level: Moderate

Path condition: Paved; width and surface vary from good to poor

Topography: Shady; forest, fields, homes, shopping centers

Usage: Lightly traveled

This path is a long, shady recreational trail built by San Mateo County Parks and Recreation for bicyclers, walkers, and equestrians (though I haven't yet seen an equestrian on the path). The ride is a steady uphill, climbing 410 feet in 4.2 miles; you can stop often to relax and enjoy the scenery on the way up. You will find the return trip a literal breeze.

Begin by taking Alpine Road south from Junipero Serra Boulevard at the western edge of Menlo Park. Park in the wide dirt area on the right side of the road just past the intersection with Junipero Serra. Carefully cross Alpine and find the bicycle path on the east side of the road. Those wishing to take a shorter ride can begin at the Ladera shopping center as described below.

The path first winds past a part of the Stanford Golf Course and then approaches Alpine Road. This northern part of the path is relatively narrow and rough. In places it is close to the roadside, and the traffic noise is irritating. However, there are several other places where the path cuts deeply through a quiet forest. In two locations, the path disappears and you must bike through a short street to pick it up again.

At the north off-ramp of the Junipero Serra Freeway (Highway 280), you have to dismount and walk your bikes. Then the path goes under the freeway and you come to a sign warning "Low Bridge, Walk Your Bikes." Actually, you can ride under this bridge, which goes under the south off-ramp, if you are careful and if you hunker down.

Continue south through a forest passing, on your left, a grassy hillside dotted with assorted large antennas known as the Stanford Antenna Farm. Most of the trees along the path are live oaks, but there are also eucalyptus, redwood, pine, maple, buckeye, and others. Pretty soon you approach the Ladera shopping center.

If you wish to take a shorter ride, park in the shopping center, carefully cross the road, and start bicycling to the south. After passing the tennis courts, the path becomes wider, smoother, and farther from the road. This central portion of the path is the best part of the ride.

You will pass a Little League park, some attractive suburban homes on the hillside, and horse corrals. The

path, which has been at a very gradual upslope, now becomes hillier.

At Arastradero Road is the Alpine Inn, a popular hamburger and beer joint, with many tables both outside and inside. The inn was originally built as a Spanish gambling house by Felix Buelna in 1852. Over the years it has had many owners; it once changed hands in a crooked poker game. It has long been a favorite hangout for Stanford students as well as weekend bicyclists.

After you leave the inn, the path becomes steeper yet. At a particularly steep, but short, upgrade, you emerge at the Alpine Hills Tennis Club (private). Now you must carefully

cross the road and continue the journey on the west side of Alpine Road. The path continues for another 0.5 mile to the corner of Alpine and Portola roads, where it ends at a small shopping center.

If you have a lot of energy left, you might wish to try the Portola Valley Ranch trail. Walk or ride your bikes 0.2 mile further south on Alpine to Indian Crossing Road, then take a left and use the wide asphalt sidewalk. The sidewalk path is very hilly and scenic. You pass a school, meadows, new homes, and a duck pond and come to the end of the path at the Portola Valley Ranch (private). There is also a bike path on nearby Horseshoe Bend Road, but it is so incredibly

Alpine Road

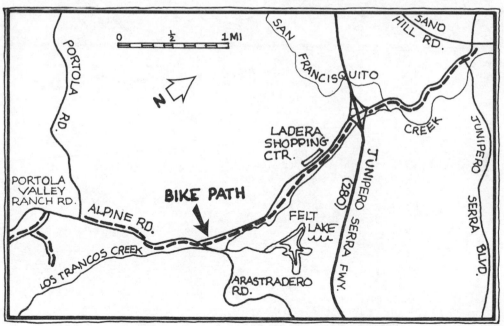

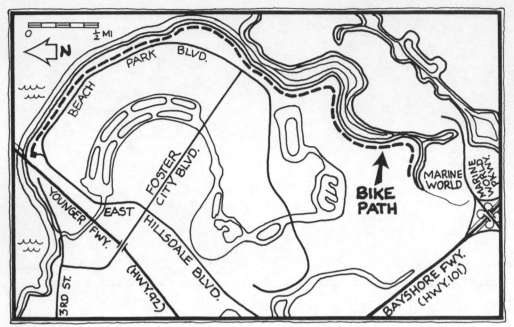

Bayfront Trail

Begin by taking the Hillsdale Boulevard exit in Foster City east from Highway 101, and drive east on Hillsdale as far as you can. As you approach the bay, the San Mateo Bridge will rise above you on your left. Look for the sign pointing to the San Mateo Fishing Pier and park in the large concrete lot on your left.

Walk your bikes past the gate; you can now turn right onto the bike path or go straight onto the fishing pier. The pier is the old San Mateo Bridge, which was replaced by the new high span structure in the early 1960s. This old bridge was a low-level, two-lane, concrete roadway with a draw-bridge in the middle. Only about 0.8 mile of the bridge remains; you can bicycle out on it if you enjoy watching fishermen or looking up at the new bridge towering high overhead.

Once you start on the bike path proper, you will find it a level, smooth path, with the bay on your left and Beach Park Boulevard about 20 feet away on your right. Across the street are many homes, a shopping center, churches, and a school.

This portion of the path is very much a part of the local community. You will probably see a number of people bicycling, skateboarding, and walking on the path. You may wish to stop at various points and walk along the shoreline or out on one of the sand spits which protrude into the bay.

After about a mile and a half, the path curves away from the roadside. You are now in the Belmont Slough Open-Space Preserve, which was dedicated by Foster City as a bicentennial project. For the next two miles, you will see a fantastic variety of bird life. On one trip, I saw gulls, swans, pelicans, herons, sandpipers,

steep that I won't even tell you what a great view you'd get if you climbed it.

After your ride, you might enjoy a visit to Lane Publishing Company, headquarters for *Sunset* magazine and Sunset Books, at Middlefield and Willow roads in Menlo Park. The Western Gardens are open Monday through Friday 8:30–4:30. Guided tours of the testing kitchens and offices are given on weekdays at 10:30, 11:30, 1, 2, and 3; free. Telephone (415) 321-3600.

Stanford Linear Accelerator on Sand Hill Road offers two-hour tours of the facility, by prearrangement, for those interested in subatomic physics. Tours are given Monday through Saturday. Telephone (415) 854-3300, extension 2204.

Bayfront Trail

Distance: 7 miles from Fishing Pier to vicinity of Marine World and return

Grade level: Easy

Path condition: Paved; wide, smooth

Topography: Open; homes, bay, marshes

Usage: Lightly traveled

The Bayfront Trail offers extensive views of the South Bay and the Belmont Slough. This is a very easy level trail which is a special treat for bird-watchers.

coots, ducks, and many species I didn't recognize.

This area is completely devoid of trees and bushes; only some marsh grasses are present. As a result, you can see for miles in any direction. This is not an unmixed blessing, since the extensive developments of Foster City and Redwood Shores are clearly visible, along with high voltage towers and industrial areas. Still, the primary environment is natural, quiet, and pleasant.

After two miles through the preserve, the pavement ends and a dirt path continues in the direction of Bayshore Freeway. If you look across the slough at this point, you will see Marine World/Africa USA. You should turn around here and return to your starting point.

The kids might enjoy a trip to Marine World, where they can see and be entertained by a variety of ocean life and African game animals. They can also entertain themselves at a super playground or a new water slide. The park is open from 9:30 to dusk daily in the summer and on weekends and holidays the rest of the year; water slide hours are 12–6 for Marine World visitors, shorter for the general public. Admission is $7.95 for adults, $4.95 for children five to twelve, under five free; water slide is $2 per half-hour for Marine World visitors, $2.75 for the general public. Telephone (415) 591-7676.

Castle Golf and Games is a smaller amusement park at 320 Bloomquist

Avenue in Redwood City (near the Harbor Boulevard exit from Highway 101). The park has pinball and videogames, three miniature golf courses, bumper boats, and a baseball batting cage. The boats cost $2 per ride, use of the batting cage costs $3; two rounds of golf cost $3 for adults and $2 for children. Open daily 11–11. Telephone (415) 367-1905.

If you don't have the time, money, or inclination for an amusement park, you can enjoy another level two-mile bicycle ride around Foster City Central Park. This park is located on a lagoon at the corner of Hillsdale and Shell boulevards.

Canada Road

Distance: 8 miles from Edgewood Road to Highway 92 and return

Grade level: Moderate

Path condition: Two-lane paved highway; very smooth

Topography: Partly shaded; hills, reservoir

Usage: Heavily traveled but uncrowded

This bicycle path exists only seven days each year: From 9:00 A.M to 4:00 P.M. on the third Sunday of each month, from April through October, the San Mateo County Parks and Recreation Department closes a stretch of Canada Road to automobile

Canada Road

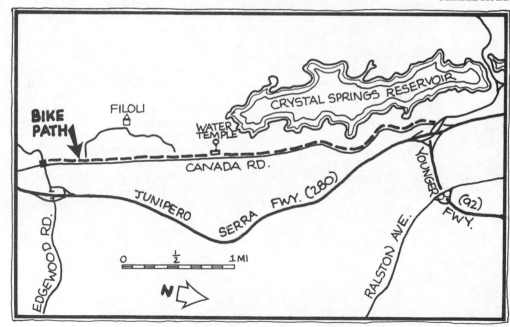

traffic. "Bicycle Sunday" is a very popular day with local bicyclists. Try it and you'll see why—this is one of the most beautiful bicycle rides in the Bay Area.

Begin by driving west on Edgewood Road from Freeway 280 in Woodside. There is ample parking available at the intersection of Edgewood Road and Canada Road.

Bike north on Canada. The path goes through the San Francisco State Fish and Game Refuge. You will be going up and down grass-covered hills, alternately in sunlight and shade from occasional eucalyptuses. Although you will have a lot of company on your trip, the road is wide enough to accommodate everybody nicely; you won't feel crowded at all.

After 1.3 miles, you pass a road leading off on your left to Filoli, the estate of the shipping heiress Lillian Matson Roth. Filoli (a combination of fight, love, and life) was built in 1916 by Willis Polk. The forty-three-room house and gardens, which are now operated by the National Trust for Historic Preservation, were used in the filming of the movie *Heaven Can Wait.* The public can tour the house and grounds Tuesday through Saturday at 10 and 1; reservations are required; admission is $3 for the garden tour and $5 for the combined tour. Children under twelve aren't allowed on the tours. Telephone (415) 366-4640 for recorded information or (415) 364-2171 for reservations; or write to Filoli Center, Canada Road, Woodside, CA 94062.

After another 0.4 mile, you come to the Pulgas Water Temple and nearby Crystal Springs Reservoir. The Hetch Hetchy Aqueduct, which brings water from Yosemite National Park to San Francisco and its environs, ends at this reservoir. The temple is a handsome classical Greek structure in which the visitor has a dramatic view of the incoming water. The well-landscaped temple grounds are a popular and pleasant spot for sunbathing, picnicking, and picture taking.

Leaving the temple, you view Crystal Springs Reservoir on your left. From here on up to Highway 92, the views of the reservoir, San Andreas Valley, and the Santa Cruz Range are spectacular.

The remainder of Canada Road continues to roll up and down the hills until you reach Highway 92. If you wish to go still further, take the Ralston Cutoff described in a later section of this chapter; otherwise head back to Edgewood Road.

The Woodside Store Museum at 471 Kings Mountain Road in Woodside was built in 1854. Over the years, it has been used as a library, dentist's office, post office, and general store. It is now a museum, stocked and furnished like a general store of 1850. Open Wednesday through Sunday 10–12 and 1–5; free. Telephone (415) 851-7615.

Huddart Park at 1100 Kings Mountain Road has an archery course, hiking and nature trails, campsites and playgrounds. Open daily during daylight hours; parking is $2 per car. Telephone (415) 364-5600.

Coyote Point Park

Distance: 4.2 miles from Third Avenue through Coyote Point Park loop and return

Grade level: Moderate

Path condition: Paved; wide, smooth

Topography: Partly open, partly deep forest; bay, park

Usage: Medium traveled

Coyote Point Park in San Mateo is a very popular place for picnicking, swimming, beachcombing, or enjoying the fine nature museum. You can select a pleasant easy ride suitable for young children or combine it with a hillier ride through a cool eucalyptus forest.

Entrance to the park is $2 per car, but, as usual, there's a way for bicyclists to get in for free. Take Third Avenue east from Bayshore Freeway (Highway 101) for a half-mile. Just after the road curves sharply to the right, look for a mini-park on your left. Park in the small dirt area near the gate just beyond the minipark and walk your bikes past the gate.

You are now on a section of the Bayfront Trail, which the county plans to extend from San Francisco to Palo Alto some day. This section is built on a levee at the edge of the bay. The trail is very wide, smooth, and perfectly level; there is no foliage. On your left about 50 yards away is a residential district; on your right are high voltage lines and the bay. After 0.9

mile, the pavement ends for a short distance and you follow a gravel path to the park boundary.

You pass through another gate to enter the park. Walk your bikes across the road toward the marina. Then walk to the left around the base of the marina to the group picnic area. If you wish to avoid any uphill bicycling, you can lock your bikes in the rack and make the rest of the trip on foot. Whether riding or walking, take the bike path, which is to the left of the group picnic area when you face directly away from the marina. This path follows fairly closely to the park entrance road, winding up and down hills in a eucalyptus forest. Soon you hear the sounds of the rifle range; then you see it. The range is open Wednesday through Friday 1–9, Saturday and Sunday 11–7; adults $3, people under nineteen $2. Telephone (415) 573-2557.

Continue paralleling the main park drive past the entrance station and back into the sunlight. Just past the entrance station, you will see a playground area off to your right. Take one of the network of bicycle paths to get there.

This is an extremely imaginative playground. The kids will enjoy walking across chain bridges, swinging on tires, walking up footsteps sunk into concrete, as well as using more conventional play equipment. While they are playing, the adults can watch airplanes on their approach into San Francisco Airport.

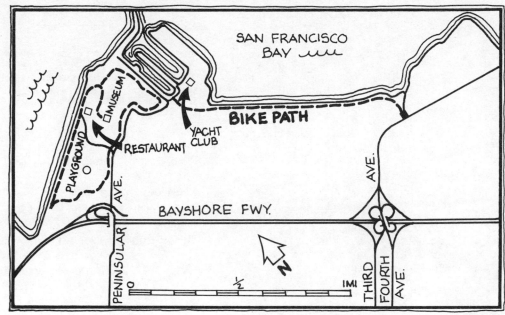

Coyote Point Park

Leave the playground area and go toward the bay, where you will find a broad paved promenade fronting on a sand beach. As you go east along the promenade, it becomes more and more crowded to the point where you may have to walk your bikes past the bathers. This beach is one of the few saltwater swimming spots on the peninsula, featuring a bathhouse, showers, restrooms, and lifeguards; free to park visitors; open daily 7:00 A.M. to 6:00 P.M. Telephone (415) 573-2592.

From the east end of the promenade, continue up a narrow, paved walking path past the Castaway Restaurant, a popular restaurant serving Polynesian food in an exotic setting. The walking path continues up a very steep bluff. Before climbing too far, you may want to leave your bikes and walk down the cliff for some secluded beachcombing. Then return to your bikes and follow the path up the hillside to a World War II memorial at the crest.

At the memorial, you rejoin a bike path. Turn to your right when facing away from the bay, and you will soon coast down to the Coyote Point Museum.

The museum has a small outdoor zoo with native animals—raccoons, foxes, coyotes, badgers, hawks, owls. You will be able to get very close to these animals. Inside are smaller animals—snakes, rodents, frogs—in cages and a number of exhibits describing the ecology of the area. There is also a small gift shop with reasonably priced items. The museum is open Tuesday through

Friday 9–5, Saturday and Sunday 1–5; free. Telephone (415) 573-2595.

From the museum, go back past the memorial and then whiz downhill toward the boat launching ramp at the north end of the marina. From here, you follow the bicycle path alongside the marina south to the point where you entered the park. Then take the levee path back to Third Street and your car.

How about a tour after the ride? San Francisco International Airport offers an interesting free tour of airport operations. Tours can be arranged on weekdays and Saturdays by appointment; telephone (415) 876-2217. The U.S. Weather Bureau at the airport also offers free tours daily by appointment. Telephone (415) 876-2886. The Rod McLellan Company, at 1450 El Camino Real, South San Francisco, offers free tours of their huge orchid growing and distributing facility daily at 10:30 and 1:30; reservations required for groups of more than three; free. Telephone (415) 871-5655.

Ralston Cutoff

Distance: 3.5 miles from Ralston Avenue and Highway 92 to Canada Road, back to Ralston, to Fox School, and return

Grade level: Difficult

Path condition: Paved; wide, fairly rough

Topography: Open; grassy hillsides, freeways, school, reservoir

Usage: Very lightly traveled

The Ralston Cutoff is a short, but very steep, path connecting Canada Road at the Crystal Springs Reservoir with Ralston Avenue in upper Belmont. The total climb is 370 feet in a distance of 1.7 miles. The trip may be taken either alone or together with the Canada Road trip on Bicycle Sunday. This ride combines good exercise, fine scenery, and a complete absence of crowds.

To get there, take Highway 92 east from Freeway 280. Take the first exit to Ralston Avenue. The exit ramp ends at a stoplight. Instead of turning here, drive directly across Ralston and park in the large dirt lot next to the road. This lot normally contains a number of cars for sale by their owners.

Take your bikes past the gate onto the path leading downhill. The grade is quite steep, dropping 170 feet in 0.4 mile. You are in the San Francisco State Fish and Game Refuge; on your left is a grass-covered hillside; on your right is Highway 92. Even though the path comes close to the freeway ramp, the traffic noise is not too bad because of the grade separation, the foliage, and the fact that these freeways don't carry a lot of large trucks.

At the bottom of the hill, the path curves to the left, paralleling Freeway 280. As you go south, the path slopes up gently until you reach a bicycle bridge across the freeway. This bridge is about 25 feet above the roadway and is totally screened in. You may wish to stop and watch the traffic speeding beneath you.

After you leave the bridge, the path descends another 80 feet to Canada

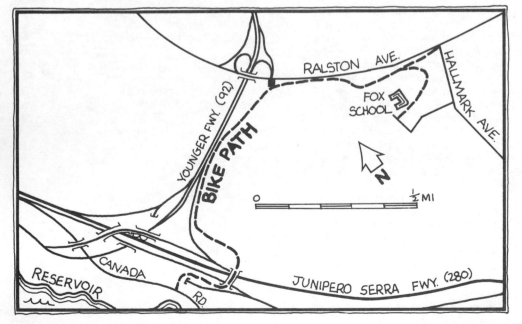

Road. This section combines an interesting maze of freeway ramps with views of the beautiful Crystal Springs Reservoir. At Canada Road, there is a gravel path leading toward the reservoir. Unfortunately the reservoir is not open to the public, and a double barbed-wire fence prevents access. Just relax here and save your energy for the return trip.

While climbing back to Ralston, you will have ample opportunity to look around. Note the almost total absence of trees. There are a number of wild licorice plants and a field of cattails, as well as wildflowers and wild grasses. When you get back to the parking lot, you may decide that you have had enough bike riding for one day.

If you decide to continue, however, follow the wide, paved sidewalk east on Ralston. This sidewalk climbs fairly gradually for 0.2 mile and then swings away from the road. Now you pass beneath a water tower on the brow of the hill to your right. Then the path climbs steeply again, climbing another 70 feet. From the top of the ascent, you have a good view of Belmont, the bay, and Mount Diablo.

After the path levels out, look for a path branching off to the right. Take this side path, and you suddenly find yourself on the grounds of Fox School. The school has a large grass area, ideal for a picnic. Right next to the school is a small, attractive public playground, as well as a concrete playground, with climbing and sliding equipment made of natural wood. This is a pleasant spot to catch your breath before the downhill run back to your car.

After the isolated ride on Ralston, you may be happy to have a more populous after-the-ride activity. If so, visit Central Park in San Mateo. The park, located at Fifth and El Camino Real, has extensive playgrounds, tennis courts, ballfields, a beautiful Japanese tea garden, outdoor entertainment on summer Sundays, and a miniature train ride.

Ralston Hall, the preserved summer mansion of the financier William Ralston, is furnished in "steamboat gothic," with crystal chandeliers and parquet floors. Located on the campus of the University of Notre Dame in Belmont, the house is open for free tours by appointment; telephone (415) 593-1601. A 1 mile nature trail leads from the house to Belmont's Twin Pines Park.

Sawyer's Camp Road

Distance: 9.6 miles from Crystal Springs Road to San Andreas Dam and return; 15.6 miles from Crystal Springs Dam to Skyline Boulevard and return

Grade level: Moderate, with two difficult hills near San Andreas Dam

Path condition: Paved; wide, smooth, very well maintained

Topography: Mostly shady; forests, lakes

Usage: Lightly traveled

This is a long ride between two beautiful reservoirs in the San Andreas Valley. The path goes through a deep forest, providing a far greater sense of isolation than bicycle riders can usually experience. You can have either a fairly easy ride or a difficult one depending on how far you go.

If you are coming from San Francisco or the North Peninsula, take the Hayne Road–Black Mountain Road exit west from Freeway 280. Then go south on Skyline Boulevard, which parallels the freeway, to Crystal Springs Road. If you are coming from the south, take the Bunker Hill Road exit from 280 west to Skyline. Then follow Skyline north one block past the overlook at Crystal Springs Dam to the intersection with Crystal Springs Road.

At this intersection, there is a parking lot on the west side of Skyline in front of a large gate and a sign saying "Historic Sawyer's Camp Road." Since you will find no further information explaining why this road is historic, I will tell you. The following historical material is courtesy of the San Mateo County Historical Museum.

The valley was granted to Domingo Feliz, a Mexican army sergeant, in 1844. Feliz farmed and raised cattle here for several years. He later sold his land to Count Haraszthy, a Hungarian nobleman called the father of California viticulture. Haraszthy found the climate too foggy for Zinfandel grapes and moved to Sonoma, where he achieved success and fame.

About 1855, the elegant Crystal Springs Hotel was built, approximately at the current site of Crystal Springs Dam. The hotel was a stage

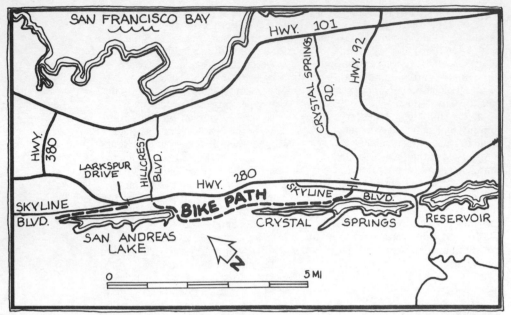

Sawyer's Camp Road

stop on the San Mateo to Half Moon Bay and Pescadero route, and was also a vacation resort for wealthy San Franciscans. Live quail were purchased by the hotel cooks for $2.50 a dozen to provide the guests with their Sunday champagne and quail brunches.

In 1868, Leander Sawyer, a circus horse trainer who boarded his horses in the valley during the off-season, established a competitive stage line. He guaranteed to make the run from San Mateo to Half Moon Bay in 70 minutes, using the horses he raised on his ranch. But his mustangs kept breaking away and scaring the passengers, so his stage line went out of

business after only a year. It was about this time that Sawyer and some of his neighbors petitioned the county to build a new road, which was named after him.

The days of the lively and elegant life in this area were numbered when the Spring Valley Water Company began secretly buying up land. In 1868, the noted engineer Herman Schussler built San Andreas Dam; in 1873, the Crystal Springs Hotel was closed, and work began on the earthen dam located approximately where Highway 92 now crosses the reservoir. In 1877, the water company workers began clearing brush in preparation for Schussler's masterpiece, the Crystal Springs Dam. It was the largest cement dam that had ever been built and was completed in 1890. The dam is composed of many blocks

of concrete cast in irregular, interlocking geometric shapes. This method of construction provided enough strength and flexibility to withstand the 1906 earthquake.

The San Francisco Water Company bought out the private Spring Valley Company in 1930. About this time, the canyon was no longer able to supply the city's water needs, so the Hetch Hetchy system was built to bring water from the Sierra. Its waters feed into Crystal Springs Reservoir near the Pulgas Water Temple.

Go past the gate and begin biking along the wide, smooth path—actually a road used (rarely) by the Water Department and the Fish and Game Refuge. You are riding in a forest of oak, madrone, and alder close to the Crystal Springs Reservoir. Along the sides of the path grow ferns, ivy, berries, poison oak, and an enormous variety of colorful wildflowers. The path goes up and down a series of very gentle grades; even the youngest member of your group should find the bicycling easy.

Distances are painted on the pavement every mile. After about 2½ miles, you pass the north end of the reservoir and enter the San Andreas Valley. Now you pass through a deeper forest of oak, madrone, and maple—a very quiet, isolated place. You will probably see some small wildlife here; I saw many lizards, small birds, and a family of quail. There are more hills on this part of the trail, but the slopes are still gentle.

After the 4 mile marker, you have a difficult climb of 100 feet leading to San Andreas Dam, where you will find a plaque placed here at the 100th anniversary of its construction. The lake is beautiful and peaceful; if you brought a lunch, this is the place to eat it. Restrooms are available here, too. From the dam, there are excellent views north across the lake and south across the valley to the reservoir.

If you desire to keep going, you must climb another very difficult hill leading to the Junipero Serra Freeway (280) at Hillcrest Boulevard. At this corner, a historical marker commemorates the camp used by the Portola expedition after the first sighting of San Francisco Bay on November 4, 1769. Now go under the freeway and walk or ride along the frontage road with the traffic for 0.6 mile to Larkspur Boulevard, then back under the freeway again.

A fine new recreation trail has been constructed leading north from Larkspur Drive. This is a wide, smooth path close to San Andreas Lake. The path is relatively hilly, passing through a forest of eucalyptus, pine, fir, and cypress, and ending at Skyline Boulevard near the northernmost tip of the lake. Rest here for a while before returning to Crystal Springs Dam.

After the ride, you might enjoy visiting Junipero Serra County Park in San Bruno. The park has several hiking trails with panoramic views, a nature trail, barbecue pits, shuffleboard, volleyball, and horseshoe courts.

San Mateo County's Historical Museum is at 1700 West Hillsdale Boulevard on the College of San Mateo campus in the city of San Mateo. The museum has displays on the prehistory, Spanish, Mexican, and American periods of the county. Open Monday through Friday 9:30–4:30, Saturday 10:30–4:30, Sunday 12–4; free. Telephone (415) 574-6441.

6 Santa Clara County

Santa Clara County Parks and Recreation Department publishes a brochure on regional parks and recreation areas. Although the brochure has little information on bicycle paths, it is useful in locating outdoor activities in the county. Write to County of Santa Clara; Parks and Recreation Department; 70 West Hedding Street; San Jose, CA 95110; telephone (408) 299-4337.

The city of San Jose distributes a useful map titled "Existing Bike Routes in Santa Clara County," plus a brochure on Alum Rock Park. Both may be obtained by writing to City of San Jose; Department of Parks and Recreation; 151 West Mission Street; San Jose, CA 95110; telephone (408) 277-4661.

Palo Alto publishes a very readable map showing on-street and off-road bike paths in the city. Write to City of Palo Alto, Recreation Department; Lucie Stern Community Center; 1305 Middlefield Road; Palo Alto, CA 94301; telephone (415) 329-2262.

Stanford University publishes a variety of maps and brochures about the campus. You may pick these up at the Information Office at the Main Quad, at Hoover Tower, or by writing to Office of Public Affairs; Building 170; Stanford University, Stanford, CA 94305; telephone (415) 497-2862.

This chapter includes descriptions of six bicycle paths in Santa Clara County. They are:

1. Alum Rock Park: One moderate and one difficult path through the historic park in the hills east of San Jose

2. Bol Park: An easy path past homes, schools, and parks in Los Altos and Palo Alto

3. Coyote Creek: A long, easy ride through a rural area south of San Jose

4. Frenchman's Hill: A moderate, secluded ride through a residential section in the hills behind Stanford

5. Los Gatos Creek: An easy path through a linear park in Campbell

6. Stanford University: An easy ride over a network of paths crossing the shady campus

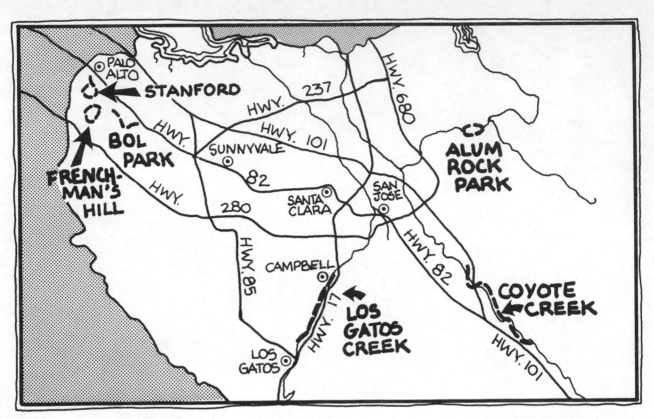

Santa Clara County

In addition to these six, there are several shorter paths in the county. Palo Alto has a new path along Arastradero Road from Foothill Expressway to Purissima Road. Sunnyvale has a level path along the Hetch Hetchy Aqueduct from Orchard Gardens Park to Fairwood School. Los Altos has a sidewalk path along Fremont Avenue from Highway 85 to Grant Road. Saratoga has a sidewalk path from Big Basin Way along Saratoga–Los Gatos Road to Fruitvale Avenue and then along Fruitvale to West Valley College.

Alum Rock Park

Distance: 2.8 miles on Woodland path from Alum Rock Avenue entrance to mid-canyon area and return. 4.4 miles on Creek path from Penitencia Creek Road entrance to mid-canyon and return.

Grade level: Woodland path—difficult; Creek path—moderate

Path condition: Woodland—paved, wide, smooth; Creek—partly paved, partly hard-packed dirt, narrow

Topography: Well shaded; park, canyon, hills

Usage: Lightly traveled on both trails

Alum Rock Park is one of the most pleasant bicycle paths in the Bay Area. The ride combines good exercise, solitude, scenery, and history. There are two separate trails in the park—Woodland path and Creek path. Though you could do both in one day, it is worth planning two or more outings to this interesting park.

Alum Rock Park was founded in 1872 as the Alum Rock Reservation. From 1890 to 1932, the park was a nationally known health spa, with twenty-seven mineral springs. The visitor could enter the park on a steam railroad to enjoy its mineral baths, swimming pool, tea garden, restaurant, and dance pavilion. Eventually overuse caused severe damage to the environment, and the facilities could not be properly maintained. Today the staff is emphasizing family outdoor activities which protect the terrain and its natural inhabitants. No food is available in the park, so bring your own.

Begin the Woodland ride by driving east on Alum Rock Avenue in San Jose. Admission to the park is $1.25 per car, but bicyclists can get in free. At the corner of Alum Rock and Canyon Vista Road, look for a small dirt parking lot on your right. Park in the lot or on one of the side streets and take out your bikes. The Woodland bike path is on your right; it is a wide, paved fire road, with a barrier to discourage motorized vehicles. Upon passing the barrier, you enter the park.

The path is quite steep; you will climb 160 feet in a distance of 0.5 mile. If you find it strenuous, take frequent rests. You will enjoy the shade of oak, madrone, and buckeye, and, because this area has very few visitors, you may see black-tailed deer, rabbits, or quail.

The summit of the path is 730 foot high Inspiration Point. Leave your bikes on the grassy knoll and walk up the short path to the point, where you can sit on a bench and admire a splendid view of Penitencia Creek Canyon and the Santa Clara Valley. If you sit here for a while, you may see a red-tailed hawk or turkey vulture circling above the canyon.

After you leave Inspiration Point, it is all downhill (130 feet) to the mid-canyon area of the park—enjoy the ride! The mid-canyon area is the heart of the park. It is usually extremely crowded with picnickers, walkers, bicyclers, frisbee throwers, and so on.

Turning to the right when you reach the canyon floor, you will soon arrive at the mineral springs area. The springs, which are housed in stone grottoes, have seven varieties of mineral water, including soda, sulphur, magnesia, and iron. Though the fountains are just trickles today, the water is potable; if you can get by the smell, taste it. The last time my family went to the park, we met some people who were filling bottles with their favorite variety.

If you wish to continue up the creek, the path remains paved for 0.3 mile. Then a hard-packed dirt path continues for another 0.4 mile to the confluence of Arroyo Aguague and Penitencia Creek. The creek has water the entire year round, and it is very pleasant to sit on the rocks and cool your feet. From the end of the path, a trail leads upstream to the scenic main falls. If you don't wish to take this side trip, then just visit the Youth Science Institute and Visitor Center before heading back up the Woodland path.

Alum Rock Park

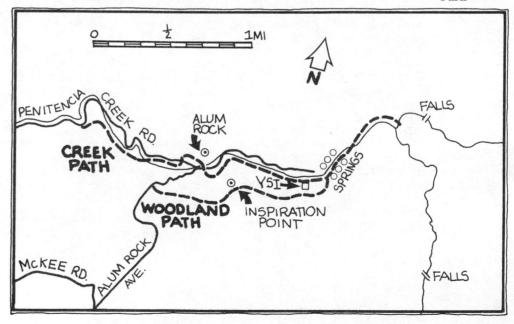

The Creek trail bicyclers can also enter the park without paying. Approach from San Jose or Milpitas on Penitencia Creek Road. Just past Poppy Lane is a dirt parking area on your right. Walk your bikes up the gravel path to the top of the hill in front of you where the trail begins.

The Creek trail is hard-packed dirt and fairly narrow, following the creek closely. It is very well shaded with oaks, fragrant bay trees, maples, and alders. While the trail does climb 220 feet in 2 miles, the slope is relatively gradual and not difficult.

This trail follows the route of the old steam railway, which was electrified in 1901. Interpretive overlooks describe the history of this railroad and point out traces, bridges, trestles, and abutments. Try to imagine riding the train from 26th and San Carlos streets in San Jose to Little Yosemite, as the park was called.

After crossing a wooden bridge over a little concrete spillway, the path seems to end at Penitencia Creek Road near the Eagle Rock picnic area. The path resumes on the other side of the road about 0.2 mile to the east. To get to the next section, bicycle through the dirt parking lots on the right side of the road until you approach the corner where Penitencia Creek Road meets Alum Rock Avenue. Cross Penitencia Creek Road just before this corner and work your way up to the old railway bridge that parallels the road on the left. Cross this bridge and look at Alum Rock, the huge mass of yellowish rock that gave the park its name. Then continue another half mile until the path becomes paved near the mid-canyon area.

The Visitor Center, another 0.3 mile after the start of the paved section, can provide information, group reservations, and first aid; it also has several educational displays. Open Monday through Friday 8–4:30, sometimes on weekends. Telephone (408) 259-5477.

The Youth Science Institute (YSI) sponsors naturalist activities for youngsters and has several educational displays and a mini-zoo, an indoor room with a number of local animals in cages and several birds of prey which are uncaged. Walking around under the watchful eyes of hawks and eagles is a unique experience. Open Tuesday through Friday 9–4:30, Saturday 12–4:30, summer Sundays 12–4:30; adults 25 cents, children 10 cents. Telephone (408) 258-4322.

After the ride, a fun place to take children is Kelley Park at Keyes Street and Senter Road in San Jose. The park is the site of San Jose Zoo. Also in the park is Happy Hollow Children's Park, with storybook settings, excellent playground equipment, rides, clown and puppet shows, and snack bars. The zoo and Happy Hollow are open Monday through Saturday 10–5, summer Sundays 11–6, winter Sundays 10–5; combined admission is $1.25 adults, 75 cents for children. Telephone (408) 292-8188. Kelley Park also has a Japanese garden with a tea house and the San Jose Historical Museum.

Lick Observatory of the University of California at Santa Cruz is 19 miles from Alum Rock Park along slow, winding Mount Hamilton Road. The visitor's gallery is open daily 10–5; guided tours of the huge telescopes and astronomical instruments are given daily 1–5. The public can also look through the telescopes on Friday nights in the summer by advance reservation. Telephone (408) 274-5061 for recorded information or (408) 429-2513 for reservations. There is no charge for these activities.

Bol Park

Distance: 3.4 miles from Los Altos Avenue to Bol Park and return

Grade level: Easy

Path condition: Paved; wide, smooth

Topography: Mostly open, some shade; homes, schools, parks

Usage: Lightly traveled

This is a level path through an attractive residential section and past several landscaped school grounds in Palo Alto and Los Altos. There are many interesting places for stopping to stroll or picnic.

To get to the path, drive south on Los Altos Avenue from El Camino Real in Los Altos. You come to the bike path in just a few blocks. While parking is allowed along Los Altos Avenue, you would be parking in an on-street bike lane. Be friendly to your fellow bicyclists and park just around the corner on Lunada or Margarita.

The path starts opposite Margarita. It is on the right-of-way of one of the feeder pipelines to the Hetch Hetchy aqueduct system. The right-of-way is a well-landscaped linear parkway with several benches for relaxing. The path is very wide, smooth, and level, but watch out for the dips when you cross Estrelita Avenue. If you take these at more than five miles an hour, all the fillings will drop out of your teeth.

After crossing Adobe Creek on a shaded wooden bridge, you leave Los Altos and enter Palo Alto. The path continues to curve through the aqueduct right-of-way. On your right are the extensive playing fields of Terman Middle School; on your left is the beautifully landscaped Alta Mesa Cemetery. Continue for 0.4 mile until you come to a busy street—Arastradero Road. Turn left on the near sidewalk and go one block past the cemetery entrance and a large apricot orchard until you come to a stoplight. Use the pedestrian button to cross Arastradero. Then follow the sidewalk on the other side of Arastradero for another block along the front of Gunn High School.

At the corner of Arastradero and Miranda Avenue, turn right. You now see the first of several barriers which have aroused the fury of Palo Alto bicyclists. Six logs have been laid on their sides to form a maze at the entrance to the bike path. The purpose, of course, is to discourage motorized vehicles. The maze is pretty effective, although mopeds can negotiate it with difficulty, but it is a big inconvenience to bicycle commuters. Walk your bikes through and continue down the path.

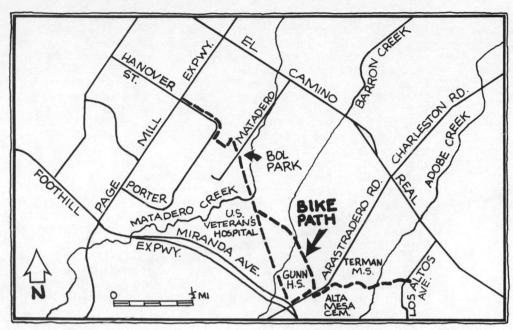

Bol Park

This part of the path follows the right-of-way of an abandoned Southern Pacific line which carried freight and passengers between Palo Alto and Vasona Junction until 1962. The path is very wide, smooth, and well maintained, with a center stripe. It starts out level but soon has some easy grades. On your left is a good view of the Stanford Industrial Park and Black Mountain.

You soon come to a sturdy bridge across Barron Creek, which flows through a marsh surrounded by a levee and spillway. Young daredevils sometimes use the levee as a bicycle obstacle course. It's really pretty safe, as these things go, if your youngsters want to try it out.

After the creek, the path goes gently downhill between the Palo Alto Veteran's Hospital and the playing fields behind Gunn High School, across Matadero Creek, to Cornelis Bol Park. The park is just a grassy area with some walnut and oak trees and a tiny playground. There are some wooden staircases leading down to Matadero Creek. The creek, which usually dries out in the summer, has a rock bed and is shaded by handsome live oaks. The children will enjoy exploring it.

The path continues beyond Bol Park, but the remainder is of more interest to commuters than to recreational bicyclists. If you do choose to continue, you must negotiate two more barriers, then follow the railroad right-of-way for one more block, finally emerging at Hanover Street in the middle of the Stanford Industrial Park. From this point, a wide sidewalk path leads west along Hanover to the corner of Page Mill Expressway, where the path ends. If you wish to have a very long bike ride, you could take this extension and then connect with one of the other paths described in this chapter. From Hanover and Page Mill, you can take the sidewalk up the very steep hill on Page Mill to connect with the Frenchman's Hill paths. Or you can take the level sidewalk along Hanover to connect with the Stanford paths.

Whether you choose to extend your bike ride or not, you will eventually return from Bol Park. On your way back, an alternate route, which avoids the one hill on this bike path, is possible. After crossing Matadero Creek, instead of going up the hill, look for the narrow paved path on your left. This path passes between the backyards of a row of suburban homes and the Gunn playing fields. The path ends at the tennis courts, and you must walk or ride your bikes through a parking lot for 0.2 mile. Then you will find a wide asphalt sidewalk path on the left of Gunn's driveway which returns you to the pedestrian stoplight at Arastradero Road. Cross the street and return along the aqueduct right-of-way.

Foothill College, located on El Monte Road just off Highway 280 in Los Altos Hills, is a good place to visit after the ride. The college has an electronics museum, with a fine collection of early radios and many do-it-yourself exhibits; open Thursday and Friday 9–4:30, Sunday 1–4:30; free but donations accepted. Telephone (415) 948-8590. The Foothill College Observatory is open for stargazing Friday nights dusk–11, and for solar viewing Saturday mornings 9–12, weather permitting; free.

NASA/Ames Research Center offers tours of their giant wind tunnel by appointment. Located at Moffett Field in Mountain View; telephone (415) 965-6497. The U.S. Navy at Moffett also offers group tours of the huge hangars and P-3 airplanes by appointment; telephone (415) 966-5976.

Coyote Creek

Distance: 12 miles from Hellyer Park to Coyote percolation pond and return

Grade level: Easy

Path condition: Paved; fairly wide, smooth, with center stripe

Topography: Generally shady; farms, orchards, park, creek, hills

Usage: Lightly traveled

This is the most rural bicycle path in the Bay Area, going through farm, orchard, and pasture land within a few miles of downtown San Jose. This is a long, level, and very uncrowded bicycle ride.

To get there, take the Hellyer Avenue offramp from Bayshore Freeway (Highway 101) in South San Jose. Bear right into Hellyer Park and park in the lot near the Velodrome. The Velodrome is an olympic-sized paved and very steeply banked oval used by bicycle racers. It may be used by permit at a cost of 50 cents for adults, 25 cents for children; bicyclists must be equipped with safety helmets and headgear. Open daily 8–4:30. Obtain permit from the Hellyer Park rangers; telephone (415) 225-0225. At any rate, look it over and then walk your bicycles back the way you drove in, through the parking lot to the start of the bike path.

The path winds past a scenic area, underneath Hellyer Avenue by some large cottonwood trees, and close to Hellyer Pond. There are a number of picnic areas by the pond, plus a snack bar, restrooms, and a playground. Usually fishermen will be trying their luck at the pond.

Leaving the park, the path goes under the freeway, then slightly up a hillside and down again. At the bottom of this hill is a little dip with a stream running across the path. There are at least a few inches of water in the stream all year long. My children love to splash around in it.

Now on your right is the creek bed, sheltered by oaks, sycamores, and maples. On your left are pasturelands, orchards, a farmhouse, and a packing house. These are usually busy with farmhands plowing, picking, or packing, depending on the time of year.

At Piercy Road, you must cross the creek on the road bridge and continue on the west bank of the creek. A few new tract homes are visible on your right, but most of this area is still devoted to vegetable fields. Soon you come to a small percolation pond, a gravel pit into which the creek water has been diverted in order to let it seep into the ground. The percolation process is used to raise the water table of the surrounding countryside.

At the time of this writing, the path is officially closed south of Tennant Road due to highway construction on the new 101 freeway which is being built to reroute traffic off San Jose's infamous "Blood Alley." The paved bicycle path still exists, however, and on weekends when construction work is stopped, you can take the path. But please be very careful about working your way underneath the freeway overpass, where the workmen have demolished the path. Hopefully construction will soon be completed and the pathway officially reopened.

The section south of Tennant Road is undeveloped open space, with much birdlife visible. The path ends at a small dam; you can walk to the edge of the spillway and watch the water pouring over it. A gravel path follows the western shore of Coyote percolation pond to Metcalf Road. After exploring the pond and relaxing, head back along the bike path to your starting point.

An interesting after-the-ride attraction is Hill Country in Morgan Hill, site of a family restaurant and a museum of aircraft, cars, wagons, and bikes. Hill Country is at 15060 Foothill Avenue; telephone (408) 227-4607. The museum is open Wednesday through Sunday 10–10; free. The restaurant is open Wednesday through Sunday 12–8:30.

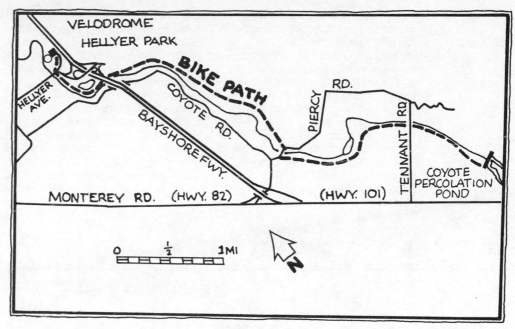

Coyote Creek

The New Almaden Museum features displays on the quicksilver mine which operated here from the 1850s to the 1940s, plus many local Indian artifacts. Located at 21570 Almaden Road in New Almaden; open Monday, Thursday, and Friday 10–4 and Saturday and Sunday 10–5 during August and September; Monday, Thursday, and Friday 1–4 and Saturday and Sunday 10–4 during October through November and February through July; closed December and January; adults $2, children six to twelve 75 cents. Telephone (408) 268-7869.

Or you could simply walk around Eastridge, a large and beautifully decorated shopping center with an ice skating rink. Eastridge is located at Capitol Expressway near Tully Road in San Jose.

Frenchman's Hill

Distance: 2.3 mile loop from Stanford Avenue and Bowdoin Street around Peter Coutts Hill, Nixon School, and return

Grade level: Moderate

Path condition: Paved; narrow, smooth

Topography: Mostly shaded; homes, schools, parks

Usage: Very lightly traveled

Frenchman's Hill is an attractive residential neighborhood located in the foothills west of Palo Alto. The neighborhood is laced with a network of walking and bicycle paths. You can enjoy a short but strenuous ride with some fine scenery. And, I can practically assure you, your group will have the paths all to themselves.

If you are approaching from Bayshore Freeway (Highway 101), take the Oregon Expressway exit west. Follow Oregon and Page Mill Expressway to El Camino Real; turn right on El Camino and left on Stanford Avenue. If you are approaching from Junipero Serra Freeway (Highway 280), take the Page Mill exit east.

Frenchman's Hill

Follow Page Mill to Peter Coutts Road; turn left and then right onto Stanford. In either case, park on the south side of Stanford at the corner of Bowdoin Street. Then cross Stanford in the crosswalk and start biking to the west on the path along the north side of Stanford Avenue.

The path cuts through a deep, mixed forest of pepper, sycamore, redwood, birch, fir, silk, and many other species. Although Stanford Avenue is only about 20–30 feet away, the trees keep you virtually unaware of its existence. The path climbs a steady slope upward; at several points, the slope becomes quite steep for a short distance. At one such point, you come to an old brick dam guarded by wildflowers and redwoods, over which water is gently trickling. This is a good place to catch your breath or to let your children look for tadpoles.

At Raymundo Avenue, cross Stanford at the pedestrian stoplight. The large building behind the grove of blue gum eucalyptus is Stanford University's Harris J. Ryan Laboratory. This huge structure was used for experiments in high-voltage physics from 1926 to 1959. In 1959 it housed the university's first nuclear reactor. Today the lab is almost deserted, used primarily for storage. You can bicycle over to the lab and peer in the windows if you like, but there isn't much to see.

Now follow the path along the left side of Raymundo Avenue up a short, steep hill and down again. At Tolman Lane, cross Raymundo and follow the path on the right side of the street. You are going through a handsome residential section on Stanford University land. The homes are mostly two-story and range from Spanish style to rustic lodges. From time to time, you will notice paved paths leading to your right and left. These are walking paths suitable for bicycling. Feel free to explore any of them; they are shady routes which skirt the beautifully landscaped homes in the neighborhood. Unfortunately, these paths don't all interconnect, and you will either have to turn around when you get to the end of a side path or else bicycle along one of the quiet side streets which lead back to Raymundo.

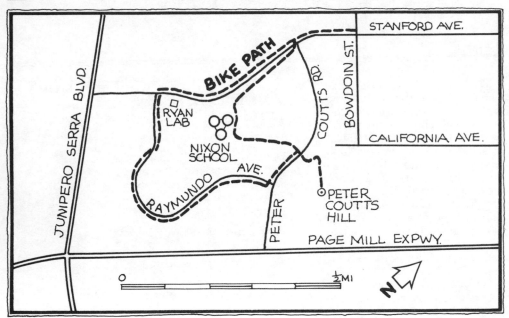

Raymundo Avenue ends at Peter Coutts Road. Turn left and take the near sidewalk path. After one block, cross Peter Coutts at the crosswalk and proceed along the paved path across the empty field to the north. You soon come to a jeep trail to the right. Walk up this trail to the crest of Peter Coutts Hill.

This windy hillside is one of my favorite places. You have a wonderful 360-degree view of Black Mountain, Palo Alto, Moffett Field, the San Francisco Bay, and the East Bay hills from Mount Diablo to Mount Hamilton. The treeless hill is covered with wild grasses, which are cut back several times a year. If you happen to be here before the spring cutting, you will enjoy the sight of a green hillside covered with purple lupine—that is, if the university doesn't decide to cover the hill with new homes.

Peter Coutts, whose name has been mentioned several times in this description, was "the Frenchman" of Frenchman's Hill. His real name, however, was Paulin Caperon. A liberal editor, he got in trouble with the Germans at the time of the Franco-Prussian War. Using the passport of his friend Coutts, he fled France, went to Switzerland, and then came to California. Between 1874 and 1880, Coutts (as I shall call him) planted trees, raised pigeons, raised thoroughbred horses, imported Ayrshire cattle, and developed a miniature lake.

One of the arched stone bridges he built to connect an island in that lake still stands in the middle of a field near the corner of Frenchman's and Estudillo roads, about a half-mile north of the bike path. He started several tunnels looking for water; Frenchman's Tower, a local landmark on Old Page Mill Road west of Foothill Expressway, was planned to contain a tank for the water he never found. Coutts returned to his native country in 1880, and Leland Stanford purchased his land to add to the Farm (see section on Stanford University).

After relaxing on the hillside for a while, return across Peter Coutts Road and up the hillside path to Lucille Nixon School, an elementary school built around the learning pod concept—several detached, octagonal clusters of classrooms. The school has playgrounds, grassy playing fields, and an obstacle course your kids will enjoy tackling. Work your way to the front of the school and then take the path just inside the chain-link fence downhill to Stanford Avenue. Then follow Stanford to your car.

After the ride, you might like to take a hike on one of the Midpeninsula Regional Open Space District trails. The district maintains a self-guiding "earthquake trail" at the Los Trancos reserve on Page Mill Road one mile east of Skyline Boulevard. To find out about the other district trails, or to arrange a docent-led nature hike, phone district headquarters at (415) 965-4717.

Palo Alto maintains an interpretive nature center at the Baylands where you can see films, hear lectures, view exhibits of the birdlife, or examine marsh creatures through microscopes. The center also has a boardwalk leading out to a platform at the bayshore from which you can see egrets, herons, pelicans, and other water birds, and a pond at which children can feed the ducks and seagulls. The center is located at the foot of Embarcadero Road; open Wednesday through Friday 2–5, Saturday and Sunday 10–12 and 1–5; free. Telephone (415) 329-2506.

Los Gatos Creek

Distance: 3.6 miles from Campbell Avenue to Los Gatos city limits and return

Grade level: Easy

Path condition: Paved; wide, smooth, with center stripe

Topography: Open; creek, ponds, freeway, parks

Usage: Lightly traveled

The Los Gatos Creek path is a short and level path with scenic views of the Santa Cruz Mountains. It combines easy bicycling with birdwatching and a par course.

To get there, take the Hamilton off-ramp east from the Nimitz Freeway (Highway 17) in Campbell. Turn right on Bascom, right on Campbell, and cross over the freeway. Then make your first left onto Gilman and find a parking space as close to the corner as you can.

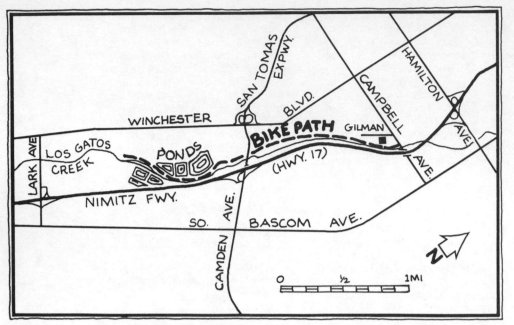

Los Gatos Creek

The path begins at Campbell Park on the corner of Campbell and Gilman. This is a small community park with lawns, picnic tables, a good playground, and a concrete roller skating circle.

Follow the path south along the west bank of the creek. Alongside is a modern spread-out par course. On your right is a light industrial area—lumber yards, maintenance yards, and the like, plus a trailer court. On your left is the creek, which has water all year long in a canyon 20 feet below you. There is a gravel path on the other side of the creek, and perhaps 50 to 100 feet on your left is the freeway. The traffic noise is quite noticeable, but not overwhelming. There

are no trees or very much in the way of vegetation except for some bushes near the freeway and a row of pungent wild licorice plants near the path.

As you leave the par course, the perfectly level path suddenly rises quite steeply. It climbs about 30 feet to the top of a spillway. You can cross the creek at a dam at the top of the spillway or just watch the people fishing. Then the path descends just as steeply as it climbed, to an underpass below the San Tomas Expressway. Be very careful here; because of the grade and narrowness of the path, walking your bikes through the underpass is advisable.

Once you climb out of the underpass, you enter Los Gatos Creek Park, a large grassy area with a number of newly planted trees; this is a pleasant place to stop for a picnic. At the south end of the park is a small lake with sailboats, ducks, and coots.

This "lake" and the two ponds next to it actually constitute the Camden Percolation System. These ponds are used to maintain the water table in the Santa Clara Valley through seepage of the water into the soil.

After you pass the third pond, there is a small dam across the creek. You may cross the creek over this dam and park your bikes at the steps of a wooden platform built between the creek and another system of percolation ponds. The platform is a quiet, shady place to sit down and observe the birdlife in the vicinity.

The path continues for only 0.2 mile more along the west side of the creek. The pavement ends at the Campbell–Los Gatos city limits, and the path continues first as a gravel path and then as a rutted dirt trail through heavy underbrush. If you've gone this far, you're in serious danger of flat tires, so it's time to turn back and return to Campbell Park the same way you came.

The Winchester Mystery House is 2 miles north on Winchester Boulevard at Freeway 280. This was the home of Sarah Winchester, inheritor of the Winchester rifle fortune. Sarah Winchester believed that she would never die as long as she continued to add to her house; the results are well worth a visit. Open Monday through Friday 9–5, Saturday and Sunday 9–5:30; adults $5.50 for the house tour, $6.50 for the house and garden tour, children (five–twelve) $3.50 for the house tour, $4.50 for the house and garden tour. Telephone (408) 247-2101.

Further north is the Rosicrucian Museum and Planetarium. This museum has an excellent collection of Egyptology—mummies, pyramids, and the like. Located at Park and Naglee avenues; open Tuesday through Friday 9–4:45, Saturday through Monday 12–4:45, closed January 1, August 2, and Thanksgiving; free. Planetarium demonstrations on Saturday and Sunday at 1, 2:30, and 4; adults $1.25, under eighteen 75 cents. Telephone (408) 287-9171.

Vasona Lake Park starts 1.5 miles south of the end of the bike path. Hopefully, the path will be extended to the park someday. The park has sailboating, fishing, picnicking, snack bars, boat rentals, and a short bicycle path. The Youth Science Institute has a branch nature center here, with exhibits, guided walks, and lectures. Open daily 12–4:30; free. Telephone the YSI at Alum Rock Park, (415) 258-4322. A short walk away, within adjoining Oak Meadow Park, you will find the narrow-gauge Billy Jones steam railroad. The railroad is open Saturday 11–5:30, Sunday 12–5:30, Tuesday through Friday in the summer 11–5:30; 50 cents per ride. Telephone Los Gatos Chamber of Commerce at (408) 354-9300.

Stanford University

Distance: 2.8 miles from Town and Country Village to Tresidder Union via Hoover Tower and return via Mausoleum

Grade level: Easy

Path condition: Paved; wide, smooth

Topography: Shady; fields, college buildings

Usage: Light to medium traveled

A vast network of walking paths, bicycle paths, and roads closed to traffic crisscrosses this beautiful campus. You will enjoy a leisurely, gentle, shady ride. If you prefer getting on a bike and riding for miles and miles, the Stanford paths may frustrate you. There are just too many interesting places to stop and look around.

Leland Stanford prospered as a merchant during the gold rush and became one of the "Big Four" who financed the transcontinental railroad. He was elected governor of California and later U.S. senator. At his country home, the Palo Alto Farm, he bred and trained trotting horses.

It was in 1884, while Leland, Jane, and their only son were on a European tour, that Leland Junior contracted typhoid fever and died. The grieving parents decided to build a university in his memory. The cornerstone was laid in 1887; the university opened in

Stanford University

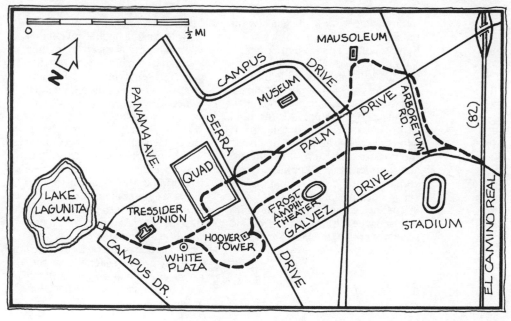

1891 with 465 students. Today Stanford University is a world-famous institution which educates approximately 12,000 undergraduate and graduate students.

From Highway 101, take Embarcadero Road west to El Camino Real in Palo Alto. From 280, take Page Mill Expressway east to El Camino, and El Camino north to Embarcadero. Then park in the lot of Town and Country Village shopping center at the corner of El Camino, Embarcadero, and Galvez Street. Walk your bikes across El Camino and start biking on the path alongside Galvez.

The asphalt path is wide and smooth, with a center stripe. To your left, across Galvez, is the 89,000-seat Stanford stadium. At the first fork in the path, stay to the left and carefully cross Arboretum Road. At this point, the path leaves the roadside and cuts through a deep, aromatic eucalyptus forest, emerging at the corner of Campus Drive and Lasuen Street.

Carefully cross Campus and take the sidewalk path alongside Lasuen, through a line of sycamores. On your left, behind a fence and hidden by the hillside, is Frost Amphitheater. If the gate is open, you should walk up and look it over. The amphitheater, used for commencements, outdoor drama, and summer concerts, is a large bowl with terraced, grass-covered benches, surrounded by approximately 150 different specimens of trees. It is an idyllic place where kids can run free and adults can relax, meditate, or study.

After leaving Frost Amphitheater, cross Memorial Way and bike on the palm-lined plaza in front of the Graduate School of Business. Then at Serra Street, turn left and head for Hoover Tower.

Hoover Tower houses the Hoover Institution on War, Revolution, and Peace. Tourist information is provided in the lobby, and there are two rooms with exhibits on the life of our thirty-first president. For 25 cents per person, you can ride the elevator up the tower for a tremendous view of the campus and the South Peninsula. Hoover Tower is open Monday through Saturday 10–12 and 1–4, Sunday 1–4. Telephone (415) 497-2862.

Leaving the tower, turn right along Serra, circumnavigate the Lou Henry Hoover Building, and turn right on a beautifully landscaped plaza. This section of the path goes gradually uphill and is apt to be somewhat crowded; in the unlikely event that you are here at class-changing time on a weekday, the bicycle traffic will be positively terrifying. Continue around the Henry Meyer Library, then turn right and make your way to White Plaza.

At the plaza is the campus bookstore, the post office, and a fountain in which my children used to wade barefoot when they were younger. Nearby is Tresidder Memorial Union, with shops, a cafeteria, and a coffee house. If you wish to continue riding a little further, take Lagunita Drive uphill from the union to the boathouse at Lake Lagunita. But be forewarned: The lake dries up each year in the spring or summer, so you are likely to see a boathouse sitting at the edge of an empty field.

When you are ready to start the return trip, head past the fountain back toward Hoover Tower. As you pass the front of the School of Education Building, look for an entranceway into the Inner Quad on your left. Enter the quad and explore its arched arcades. The classrooms are in the original romanesque buildings constructed from native sandstone in 1891. Note particularly Memorial Church, which is open to visitors daily except when services are in progress. By all means, go inside and witness its majesty.

From the church, go through Memorial Court and out across Serra Avenue. Then bicycle across The Oval, a well maintained lawn and flower garden. Proceed on the paved path on the left side of Palm Drive, a broad boulevard bordered by two long lines of stately palms.

At Museum Way, the Leland Stanford Junior Museum is one block to your left. You might wish to take a side trip there to see Stanford family mementoes, Egyptian antiquities, and the original Golden Spike which connected the transcontinental railroad in 1869. The museum features one special show in addition to the permanent collection. It is open Tuesday through Friday 10–4:45, Saturday and Sunday 1–4:45; free. Telephone (415) 497-4171.

After carefully crossing Campus Drive, make a 45-degree left turn onto a road closed to cars. This road passes through a quiet forest of oak and cedar. You soon come to the mausoleum—an elegant granite temple guarded by sphinxes—the burial place of the Stanford family. Then the road returns you to the corner of Palm Drive and Arboretum Road. Cross both streets with the stoplight and follow the shady sidewalk path along Arboretum and Galvez back to your car.

After the ride, you might like to visit some of the Stanford attractions which you passed by on your bicycles. Or you could take the student-led one-hour walking tour of the campus. This tour leaves the Information Office at the entrance to the Inner Quad, Monday through Friday at 11 and 2:15, other times by appointment. Telephone (415) 497-2862.

Another interesting attraction is the Palo Alto Junior Museum at Middlefield Road and Kellogg Avenue. The museum has a number of exhibits including a mock submarine setup; a giant camera obscura; and a small zoo with native animals, birds, and reptiles. Open Tuesday through Saturday 10–12 and 1–5, Sundays and holidays 1–4; free. Telephone (415) 329-2111.

7　Northern California

CALTRANS is a good source of bicycle information about Northern California. This agency distributes several free pamphlets including "Berkeley to Lake Tahoe Bicycle Touring Guide," "Central Valley Bicycle Touring Guide," "California Aqueduct Bikeway," "Marin County Bikeways," and "Bay Area Bike Touring Guide." They may be obtained by writing or calling Department of Transportation; P.O. Box 3366, Rincon Annex; San Francisco, CA 94119; telephone (415) 557-1840; or CALTRANS Office of Bicycle Facilities; P.O. Box 1499; Sacramento, CA 95807; telephone (916) 322-4314.

To obtain a map of the American River Parkway, contact County of Sacramento; Department of Parks and Recreation; 3701 Branch Center Road; Sacramento, CA 95827; telephone (916) 366-2061. For a map and brochure on Spring Lake Park, contact Sonoma County Regional Parks Department; 2555 Mendocino Avenue; Santa Rosa, CA 95401; telephone (707) 527-2568.

The University of California publishes maps of the Davis and Santa Cruz campuses. Obtain the first from University of California, Davis; Visitor Services and Ceremonies; Davis, CA 95616; telephone (916) 752-0539. Obtain the second from University of California, Santa Cruz; Public Information Office; Santa Cruz, CA 95064; telephone (408) 429-2495.

If you are willing to pay $4, you can get the City of Davis Bike Study from Planning Department; City of Davis; 226 F Street; Davis, CA 95616; telephone (916) 756-3740. A less encyclopedic, but still very useful—and free—map, showing bike routes in the city plus a historical bike route, may be obtained from Davis Area Chamber of Commerce; 620 Fourth Street; Davis, CA 95616; telephone (916) 756-5160.

The National Park Service publishes a brochure and a bimonthly newsletter on Yosemite Park, and a guide to "Bicycle Riding in the Western National Parks." They may be obtained from National Park Service; 450 Golden Gate Avenue; San Francisco, CA 94102; telephone (415) 556-4122; or P.O. Box 577; Yosemite National Park, CA 95389; telephone (209) 372-4461.

This chapter includes descriptions of seven bicycle paths in Northern California outside the six Bay Area counties. They are:

1. American River Parkway: An easy ride in a shady, undeveloped river valley near downtown Sacramento

2. California Aqueduct: A long, easy, sunny ride by an aqueduct at the western edge of the San Joaquin Valley

3. Lake Tahoe Bikeway: A moderate ride through a residential area on the northwest side of the beautiful lake

4. Spring Lake: A moderate ride through two lakeside parks east of Santa Rosa

5. U. C. Davis: An easy ride through an arboretum located in "the bicycle capital of America"

6. U. C. Santa Cruz: A difficult ride with splendid wide-angle views across the open campus

7. Yosemite Valley: A moderate ride through the magnificent valley in Yosemite National Park

Northern California

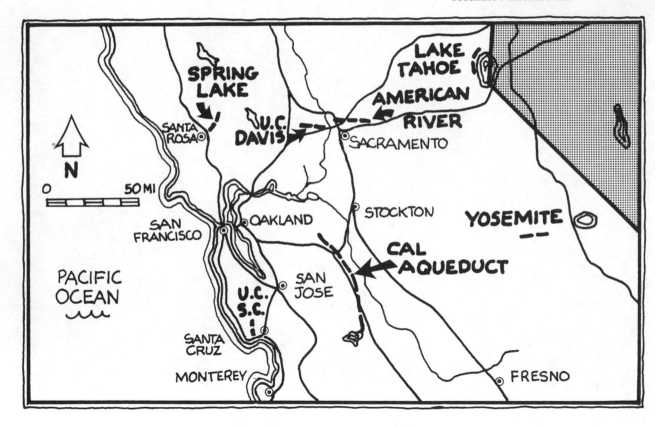

American River Parkway

Distance: 24.4 miles from Discovery Park to Rio Americano High School and return

Grade level: Easy

Path condition: Paved, with center stripe; wide, smooth

Topography: Mostly shaded; flood plain, levees, river, canals

Usage: Lightly traveled

My family makes an annual trip to Sacramento, primarily to enjoy this fine bicycle trail. It is a long but gentle ride through some pleasant riverside scenery. Even though you pass within two miles of the State Capitol, you will be in a quiet, wooded natural environment. Because of the cool breezes and deep shade, this ride is even fun in the notorious Sacramento summer.

The American River Parkway begins at Discovery Park; as we shall see below, there are many other points at which to start the ride. To get to Discovery Park, take the Richards Boulevard exit from Interstate 5. Take Richards west half a block to Jibboom Street, turn right on Jibboom, cross the American River, and you are in the park. Park your car in the large paved lot just across the bridge.

Discovery Park, at the confluence of the American and Sacramento rivers, has a boat ramp, a few walking trails, and a large grassy area for running and picnicking. It is a favorite spot for shore fishing. Before starting your ride, walk out to the point where the two rivers join and enjoy the view from the high bluffs.

The bike path, officially known as the Jedediah Smith National Recreation Trail, begins at the parking lot at a sign reading "Mile 0." Mileage signs are posted at 1 mile intervals along the length of the trail.

The path goes under Interstate 5 and then cuts away from Discovery Park Road. On your left is the wooded bank of the Natomas East Drainage Canal. Garden Highway is built on a levee on the other side of the canal, and occasionally the sound of a car passing by can be heard over the sound of birds singing. On your right is a weed-covered broad flood plain from which earth fill was taken to elevate all the streets in old Sacramento during the 1860s. At one point, you pass a noisy earth digging operation still going on.

The path is wide and smooth, with a center stripe. There is a lot of shade, mostly from large cottonwood trees along the canal. There are also oak, alder, and willows. The natural vegetation includes wild grape vines, wild berries, poppies, and lupine. For the most part, you are unaware of the city surrounding you; there are only one or two places from which a glimpse of downtown Sacramento and the capitol is possible. Along the trail at frequent intervals, you will find picnic tables, water, and restrooms.

After passing under Northgate Boulevard and crossing Del Paso Boulevard, you go under Highway 160 and the Western Pacific tracks. Now there is a branch of the canal on your right and a high levee on your left. From this point to the end of the trail, you will be well protected from traffic noise.

At the 4 mile marker, the path makes a sharp right turn and then a left turn and goes underneath Interstate 80. For the first time, you are close to the American River. The river is a good place to soak up the sun and to explore. My children were quite excited to find "fool's gold" by the riverbank. Perhaps, considering the history of this river, it wasn't fool's gold. Swimming is not recommended. The water is deep and the current strong; there have been many swimming accidents over the years.

This part of the trail is on the grounds of the California Exposition. The giant blue, white, and red "Easter egg" you see is actually the water tower for Cal Expo. Cal Expo has frequent activities, including horseracing and livestock, agricultural, and floral exhibits. Telephone (916) 924-2081 for the current schedule.

At the 6 mile marker, you pass a power station and come to a fork in the path. You can go either way; the path to the right follows the riverbank and is more scenic; the one to the left is a secluded path between the levee and a forest. The two paths rejoin at the Campus Commons Golf Course after a short distance.

From the golf course, you have the option of staying on the main trail or of following the levee. The levee is paved for the next 7 miles, but the pavement is rougher than the trail. Check which way the wind is blowing; you will be far more susceptible to wind on the levee. Another consideration is that the levee is completely unshaded. All in all, the main trail is more enjoyable, but you should plan to take the levee for part of the way either coming or going. The scenery on the levee is very different from that on the main trail—on your left is a handsome residential area with houses, apartments, shopping centers, and so on; on your right are the thickets, grasslands, and forests along the riverbank.

At the 8 mile marker you may not believe your eyes—can you have somehow reached San Francisco? No; what you see is not the Golden Gate Bridge but the Guy West Bridge, a small-scale replica of the famous San Francisco landmark. But this bridge is strictly for pedestrians and bicyclists going between student housing and the campus of California State University, Sacramento.

After passing the campus and the Sacramento Filtration Plant (the large blue and gray structure across the river), the path goes underneath Howe Avenue. The stretch of levee path between Howe and Watt has an unusual feature. The county has placed signs identifying the ground cover on the side of the levee—grasses, wildflowers, ivy, and even weeds!

At Watt Avenue, the path, which up to now has been almost perfectly level, begins to roll up and down some easy grades. You will pass through another broad flood plain, from which

the peaks of the Sierra are clearly visible. At the 12.2 mile point, the trail officially ends at Rio Americano High School. The paved levee path continues for another mile and a half to the Arden Bar area, but the pavement becomes progressively rougher, so the high school is a good place to turn back.

The county has long planned to continue the bike path beyond the high school and to cross the river at Arden Bar. The path would then connect with an existing upper part of the Jedediah Smith National Recreation Trail. However, budgetary difficulties make this plan doubtful. The upper part of the trail is 8.5 miles long on the south side of the river from C.M. Goethe Park to Nimbus Dam near Folsom.

If you don't want to take the entire 12.2 miles from Discovery Park to the high school, there are several other places at which to start and end. The following table lists all the road access points with parking.

MILEAGE FROM DISCOVERY PARK	ACCESS POINT
0.0	Discovery Park
3.6	Canterbury Road off Leisure Lane
6.0	Ethan Way just south of Hurley Way
8.1	University Avenue at Guy West Bridge
9.6	Kadema Drive at Clunie Drive
11.3	Estates Drive at Crondal Drive

After the ride, there are many things to do in Sacramento. Gibson Ranch County Park has farm animals, bike paths, a blacksmith shop, a small museum, and swimming in the summer. Located on Elverta Road near Watt Avenue; open daily 7:00 A.M. to dusk; free. Telephone (916) 366-2061.

William Land Park, located at Freeport Boulevard and Sutterville Road, has a zoo, Fairytale Town, kiddie rides, pony rides, and Japanese flowering cherry trees. The zoo is open Monday through Friday 9–4, Saturday, Sunday, and holidays 9–5; adults $1.50, children seven–twelve, 75 cents. Fairytale Town is open Tuesday through Sunday 10–5; adults 75 cents, children three–twelve, 25 cents. Telephone numbers are: zoo (916) 447-5094, Fairytale Town (916) 449-5233.

The State Capitol has guided tours weekdays at 9:30, 10:30, 1:30, and 2:30; this is a chance to shake hands with your legislators. Reservations are not required for small groups; telephone (916) 445-5200 for the legislative schedule.

Sutter's Fort at 28th and L streets is a reconstruction of the adobe house built by Johann Sutter in 1839. Self-guiding tours daily 10–5; adults 50 cents, children 25 cents. Telephone (916) 445-4209. On the same grounds as the fort is the State Indian Museum, with artifacts from all the major tribes of California. The museum is open the same hours as Sutter's Fort, has the same telephone number and is free.

The California Almond Exchange at 1802 C Street has a film and tour of an almond processing factory, Monday through Friday at 10, 1, and 2; telephone (916) 446-8402. Wonder Bread at 1324 Arden Way offers weekday tours by arrangement; telephone (916) 929-9121. Both tours are free, and the visitor is offered free samples.

And don't miss Old Sacramento. This six-block section of the city close to the Sacramento River has been restored to the way it appeared in the 1850s—complete with gas lights, board sidewalks, and cobbled streets. The area now has many restaurants, shops, and two interesting museums— a one-room schoolhouse and the Central Pacific railway station.

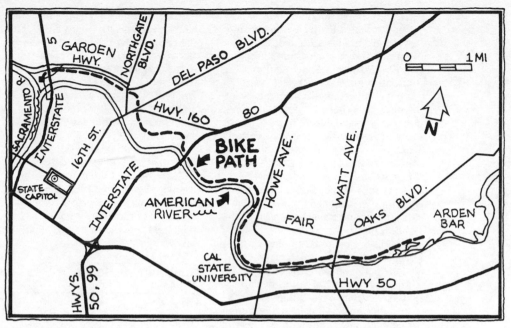

American River Parkway

California Aqueduct

Distance: Up to 131 miles round trip from Bethany Reservoir to O'Neill Forebay

Grade level: Easy

Path condition: Paved; wide, rough surface, well maintained

Topography: Open; no trees; grassy hillsides, fields, pastures, canal

Usage: Very lightly traveled

This is the longest bike path in Northern California. You can bike all 131 miles of it or any portion that you think is right for your group. It offers an easy, secluded ride. But beware of hot summer days; there is practically no shade. And bring your own drinking water.

This is the one bike path I haven't ridden in its entirety, so I will describe only the northernmost section—7.4 miles round trip from Grant Line Road to Bethany Reservoir. But I believe that the remainder of the path is similar to this section.

To get there, take the Grant Line Road exit north from Interstate 580 just west of Tracy. Bear right at the intersection of Altamont Pass Road; cross the aqueduct and park in the large gravel lot on the left side of the road. Then walk your bikes through the lot and past the barrier ingeniously designed to allow bicycles to pass with a minimum of inconvenience while prohibiting motorized vehicles.

The Grant Line area is very popular with fishermen, so you will probably see a number of people in the first 100 feet; you'll soon leave them behind. You are traveling on a wide, rough path along the east side of the aqueduct. Even though you are passing through rolling hillsides at the western edge of the San Joaquin Valley, the path is perfectly level. The hills are grass covered with few trees and many grazing cows. From time to time, you will see another canal a short distance to your right. This is the Delta-Mendota Canal, a project of the U.S. Department of Interior's Central Valley Project, which brings water from Shasta Lake down to the agricultural regions around Fresno.

The California Aqueduct is a State of California Water Project. Water from Oroville Dam is brought to Central and Southern California, where it is used for agriculture, cities, industry, hydroelectric power, recreation, and fish and wildlife protection. The bikeway was opened in 1972 by the California Department of Water Resources. According to plan, the bikeway will someday cover 400 miles from Bethany Reservoir to the Antelope Valley in Los Angeles County.

Signs are posted frequently warning the bicyclist to stay away from the aqueduct. The water flows very rapidly and the concrete sides are steep and slippery—falling in wouldn't be very healthy. The aqueduct has emergency ladders every 500 feet in case anyone does fall in. But don't get me wrong! The path is well separated from the water; as long as your group shows some common sense, your ride will be perfectly safe.

There are no trees on the path. During summer days, the sun and the insects can be bothersome. Rest stops with water and shade are provided at approximately 10 mile intervals along the bikeway, and every half-mile a marker is painted along the west wall of the aqueduct. These markers give miles and kilometers from the start of the aqueduct, which is at Clifton Court Forebay, 4.5 miles north of the start of the bikeway.

After 2.5 miles, you pass the hydroelectric station at Bethany Dam. Then the path follows the eastern shore of Bethany Reservoir another 1.2 miles to the parking area at the north end of the reservoir. At the parking area, you will find picnic tables, shade, water, and restrooms. After relaxing for a while, return to your car along the same route.

Should you choose to ride another section of the bikeway, access is possible from any of the roads (except freeways) that cross the aqueduct, but adequate parking is provided only as indicated in the following table. This table also lists the rest stops along the bikeway.

AQUEDUCT MILEAGE	PARKING AREA	REST STOP	LOCATION
0.0	No	No	Clifton Court Forebay
4.5	Yes	Yes	Bethany Reservoir (start of bike path)
8.2	Yes	No	Grant Line Road
12.0	No	Yes	Patterson Pass Road
24.0	No	Yes	Blewett Road
31.6	Yes	No	McCracken Road (Ingram Creek)
34.2	No	Yes	Howard Road
40.5	Yes	No	Sperry Road
46.0	No	Yes	Fink Road
56.9	No	Yes	Sullivan Road
61.1	Yes	No	Cottonwood Road
70.0	Yes	Yes	O'Neill Forebay

After a hot ride, one way to cool off would be to take a dip in a giant water slide. Two parks with water slides can be found near the northern end of the bikeway. The Oakwood Lake Resort at 874 East Woodward Avenue, Manteca, has eight slides, lake swimming, bumper boats, pedal boats, and jet skis. Telephone (209) 239-9566 for hours and rates. The Orchard RV Park on Maze Boulevard (Highway 132), 3 miles east of Vernalis, has two slides, a swimming pool, an RV park, restaurants, and a weekend flea market. Telephone (209) 836-2090 for more information.

If you are riding on a weekday, you could take the interesting tour of Hershey's chocolate plant in Oakdale. Tours Monday through Friday 8:15–3 at 1400 South Yosemite Avenue; free, and free samples provided. Telephone (209) 847-0381.

Miller's California Ranch is 10 miles east of Modesto on State Route 132. The ranch has a collection of old cars, trucks, bicycles, and sleighs, plus replicas of an old grocery store and barber shop. Open daily 10–5 but call ahead to make sure; adults $1, ages six to eleven 50 cents. Telephone (209) 522-1781.

If you are near the southern end of the bikeway, be sure to stop in at the Romero Visitor Center at San Luis Reservoir, 10 miles west of Los Banos. This modern, refreshingly air-conditioned structure has exhibits, movies, and slide shows on the Central Valley Project plus scenic views of the dam and reservoir; open daily 9–5. Telephone (209) 826-0718, extension 253.

You could also visit Casa de Fruta on Highway 152 near the Hollister turnoff, a commercial establishment with a playground, miniature train ride, small zoo, wine and fruit tasting, restaurant, snack bar, and Western barbecues. Telephone (408) 842-9316.

Lake Tahoe Bikeway

Distance: 12.8 miles from Timberland Lane to River Ranch Lodge and return

Grade level: Moderate

Path condition: Paved; variable width and smoothness

Topography: Shady; homes, forests, riverbank

Usage: Medium traveled

There are several paved, off-road paths on the northwest shore of this beautiful Sierra lake. You will enjoy a shady, hilly ride through the pine trees. And you can finish the trip with either an exciting raft ride down the Truckee River or a quiet drink at the River Ranch Lodge.

Start the ride from the corner of Timberland Lane and West Lake Boulevard (Highway 89), three miles south of Tahoe City. Park on Timberland close to the corner and start

bicycling to the north on the paved path along the left side of Highway 89.

The path goes through a forest of cedar and pine with some cypress and fir. It is close to the road, and you will be aware of the traffic noise. Though the path is generally level, you do go up and down some short, but steep, grades.

At Chinquapin Lane, after about a mile, carefully cross the highway in the crosswalk and follow the path on the east side. In a few blocks, the path joins a street with light local traffic. This leads downhill to a beach and then up a long grade back to the highway.

As you approach Tahoe City, you again cross the highway, and go up and down a steep hill. You continue along the sidewalk path through a residential section until the path ends about a quarter-mile short of the Tahoe City Y—the intersection of Highways 89 and 28. Walk or ride your bikes along the roadside and across Fanny Bridge, the only outlet from the lake. There are usually many people standing on the bridge watching the large trout going through the outlet gates.

At the Y, turn left on Lake Tahoe Boulevard (staying on Highway 89). After 0.1 mile, a paved path starts on the left side of the road. This path remains between the highway and the Truckee River for the remainder of the route, a distance of 3.4 miles.

The path is wide, smooth, and generally level, but with a slight downhill grade. You are still in a conifer forest, with an occasional birch tree and heavy brush along the riverbank. You can approach the river in many places for wading and can swim in a few spots. The river is generally crowded with rafters paddling downstream.

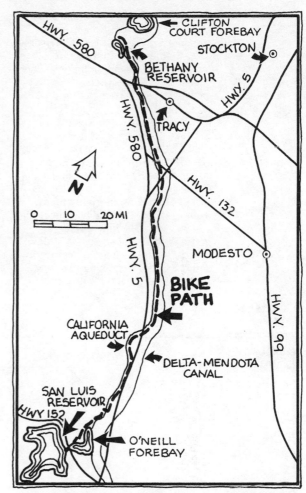

California Aqueduct

The path ends at the roadside within walking distance of the River Ranch Lodge. The lodge is a good place to relax and have a meal, snack, or drink before returning to your car.

If you want to try rafting, there are two concessionaires located at the

Tahoe City Y. Rafters paddle downstream to the River Ranch and are transported back by bus. The river is safer than most California raft routes, but there are several potentially dangerous spots; be sure that everyone can swim. For rates and times, contact Mountain Air Sports, (916) 583-5606, or Truckee River Raft Rentals, (916) 583-9724.

The Ponderosa Ranch on Highway 28 at Incline Village, Nevada, is a commercial establishment at which episodes of the Bonanza TV series were filmed. The ranch features a frontier village, museum, stagecoach and wagon rides, kiddie rides, and petting farm. Open daily 10–5 May through October, weather permitting; adults $4, children under twelve $3. Telephone (702) 831-0691.

Regularly scheduled cruises to Emerald Bay leave the Ski Run Marina in South Lake Tahoe daily, weather permitting. Contact Miss Tahoe Cruises, (916) 541-3364, or Lake Tahoe Cruises, (916) 541-4652, for schedule and rates. There are also cruises from Zephyr Cove on the Nevada side of the lake to Emerald Bay. Contact Woodwind Sailing Excursions, (702) 588-6121, or the *M. S. Dixie* paddlewheeler, (702) 588-3508 for information.

The Stateline Fire Lookout has a self-guided nature trail and a panoramic view of North Lake Tahoe. Take Reservoir Drive uphill from the North Shore Club in Crystal Bay, 12 miles northeast of Tahoe City. The lookout tower is sometimes open to the public. Telephone Visitor Information Service, (916) 583-3642, for information.

The U.S. Forest Service has a visitor center on Highway 89 near Camp Richardson with exhibits, self-guided trails, ranger-led hikes, and the Stream Profile Chamber, where you can get a unique view from below the surface of a mountain stream. The chamber is open daily 9–5 from June 15 to Labor Day, closed December 2 through April 15, open Wednesday through Sunday 10–4 the rest of the year; free. Telephone (916) 541-0209.

Vikingsholm is a reproduction of a ninth-century Viking castle. The thirty-eight-room home is open for free tours daily 10–4, June 1 to Labor Day. The castle is reached by a 1 mile hike, descending 400 feet from Highway 89 at Emerald Bay.

Spring Lake

Distance: 2.3 mile loop around the lake, or 3.9 miles with side trip to Howarth Park

Grade level: Moderate

Path condition: Paved; wide, smooth, well maintained

Topography: Partly shady, partly open; parks, lakes, forests, hills

Usage: Medium traveled

This is a very scenic ride in the foothills east of Santa Rosa. You will have a combination of level and hilly riding through a county and city park with many interesting facilities.

To get there, take Highway 12 east from Highway 101 in Santa Rosa.

Lake Tahoe Bikeway

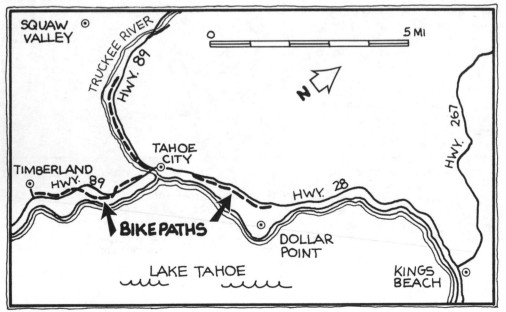

Turn right on Montgomery Drive, and follow Montgomery for 2.5 miles to Channel Drive. On the way to Channel, you will notice a number of cars parked near the main dam. While you could park here and hike into the park, this is not a convenient means of entry for bicycles. Instead, turn right on Channel, and right again on Violetti Drive to the park entrance. Parking at Spring Lake County Park is $1.50 per car, but bicyclists can get in free by parking on Violetti or Pepperwood Drive and walking or riding in. If you have smaller children, I recommend paying the fee and driving down to the parking lot at the lakeshore.

Spring Lake Park was designed and constructed by the Sonoma County Water Agency and opened for public use in 1974. This park connects Santa Rosa's Howarth Park and the state's Annadel Farms Park in a continuous greenbelt. The 75 acre lake is used as a floodwater storage reservoir. The recreational facilities are maintained and operated by the Sonoma County Regional Parks Department under contract with the Water Agency.

Start your ride on the paved bike path to the right of the parking lot by the lake. The path is very wide and smooth and perfectly level. There is a modern spread-out par course along the path, so expect lots of company. The county has planted a line of young trees—redwood, willow, alder, elm—along the shore, but they don't provide much shade yet.

Soon the path dips as you cross a diversion channel. Then you climb a steep, but fairly short, slope up to the main dam. From the crest of the dam, you get a fine view of the valley, lake, and nearby hills. It is usually windy here; I hope the wind is at your back as the path follows along the crest of

the dam for a short distance and then descends another steep slope back to the lakeside.

After leaving the dam, notice the many oak trees with Spanish moss growing on them. As you round the northwest corner of the lake, you pass by a marshy area much favored for fishing; the lake is stocked with bass, trout, and bluegill.

You soon come to a fork in the path. Those desiring a shorter ride should bear left and continue around the lake; those desiring a longer ride should bear right and take a side trip to Howarth Park.

The path to Howarth Park first climbs steeply up to the West Saddle Dam, then goes through a cool, hilly oak and madrone forest. The path emerges from the forest at the shore of Lake Ralphine and follows the lakeshore to the park.

Howarth Memorial Park is a popular Santa Rosa city park which features picnic grounds, barbecue pits, snack bars, fishing, rental boats, and two well-furnished playgrounds. The younger kids will enjoy a merry-go-round, pony rides, and a miniature train ride, each costing 15 cents per ride. There is also a barnyard here with pettable animals. The park is open daily. The rides are open 11–4,

Spring Lake

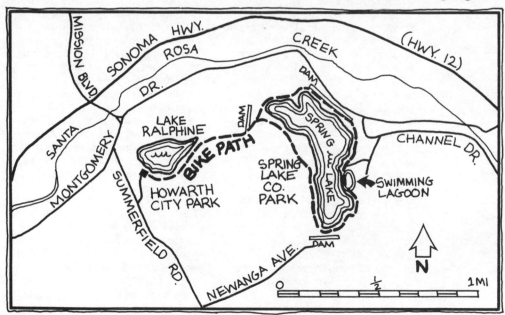

Tuesday through Sunday during summer vacation, weekends only during the school year. Telephone (707) 528-5115. After enjoying the amenities, return along the path to Spring Lake Park.

Taking the left-hand path from the fork at Spring Lake, you climb a fairly steep hill and pass some basalt rock outcroppings and several huge water storage tanks. The path ends temporarily at the access road to the Jack Rabbit Meadows Picnic Area. From this point, walk or ride your bikes straight ahead along the road until you come to a T junction. Then turn left and go downhill to the boat launching ramp. Rental boats are available in the summer.

The path starts again from the ramp, along the lake. There are some wild boysenberries and coyote bush along this section. You soon reach another fork, with a side path leading up to the South Saddle Dam and the nearby picnic grounds and campgrounds. The lakeside path continues across another diversion channel to the swimming lagoon.

The 3 acre swimming lagoon is spring fed by 85-degree temperature water. Swimming season is from about Memorial Day to Labor Day; showers, changing rooms, and lifeguard service are provided, and there is a snack bar nearby. For swimming or general park information, telephone (707) 539-8092.

After the swimming lagoon, you come to the parking lot at which you began your loop of the lake.

Santa Rosa has a number of interesting after-the-ride attractions.

Robert Ripley, author of the "Believe-It-or-Not" comic strip, was a Santa Rosa native. The Ripley Memorial Museum contains curios, cartoons, and other memorabilia. It is located in a church made from a single redwood tree, constructed in 1873 in Julliard Park at Santa Rosa and Sonoma avenues; open daily May through September 11–5, open daily October through April 11–4; adults 50 cents, children nine to seventeen 15 cents.

The famous horticulturist Luther Burbank also lived in Santa Rosa. The Luther Burbank Memorial Gardens display many of his agricultural experiments. Located on Santa Rosa Avenue across the street from Juilliard Park, the gardens are open daily 24 hours and are free; the home is open for tours Tuesday through Sunday 12–4; 50 cents per person. Information on the Ripley and Burbank attractions is available by telephoning (707) 528-5115.

A current resident of Santa Rosa is Charles Schulz, creator of the "Peanuts" comic strip. Mr. Schulz is part owner of the Redwood Empire Ice Arena, which is decorated in a Peanuts motif. This public skating rink, located at 1667 West Steele Lane, is open Tuesday, Thursday and Friday 4–5:30, Tuesday and Thursday 7:30 P.M. to 9:30 P.M., Friday and Saturday 8:00 P.M. to 11:00 P.M., Saturday and Sunday 12:30–5; adults $3, twelve to seventeen years old $2.50, under twelve $2, skate rental 75 cents. Telephone (707) 546-7147.

Going to the east from Spring Lake on Highway 12, you soon enter the Valley of the Moon area. The Jack London State Historical Park in Glen Ellen contains the author's ranch,

home, grave, and the ruins of his twenty-six-room mansion, Wolf House. Open daily 10–5; parking $2. Telephone (707) 938-5216.

Sonoma State Historic Park is located at the plaza in downtown Sonoma. The park includes a number of historic buildings—Mission San Francisco Solana, General Vallejo's city home and gardens, the Sonoma barracks, and several old inns and wineries; open daily 10–5; adults 50 cents, children 25 cents. Telephone (707) 938-4779.

One mile south of Sonoma on Broadway, you will find Train Town, a 10 acre forested railroad park. The park features a 15 minute ride on a small-scale steam railroad; open daily 11–5 in summer, weekends rest of year. The fare for the first ride is adults $2.50, children $1.50; subsequent rides are half-price, good for three months. Telephone (707) 938-3912.

U.C. Davis

Distance: 3.2 mile loop from Putah Creek Lodge to railroad tracks and return

Grade level: Easy

Path condition: Paved; smooth, varies from wide to narrow

Topography: Shady; creek, ponds, school buildings

Usage: Lightly traveled

This is a leisurely ride through a shady arboretum. You will enjoy identifying trees, feeding the ducks, having a picnic on the grass, or meeting the friendly people of Davis.

ing the friendly people of Davis.

The Davis campus of the University of California was opened in 1908. It was known as the University Farm because it was strictly an agricultural school academically affiliated with U.C. Berkeley. Since 1951, it has been an independent unit of the University of California, offering a full liberal arts curriculum but most famous for its schools of agriculture, winemaking, and veterinary medicine.

Although the students used bicycles extensively, by 1960 automobile traffic made the bicycle as endangered a species in the city of Davis as it was anywhere else. At that time, a citizen's group was formed, and in 1966 pro-bikeway candidates won the city election. Since then, the city has built bikeways along all the major streets, as well as a network of off-road paths, and has encouraged their use by both commuters and recreational cyclists. Today Davis is called the bicycle capital of America: the city has 36,000 people and 30,000 bicycles.

Begin this ride by taking the Old Davis Road exit north from Interstate 80. Follow Old Davis to the edge of the campus, then turn left on La Rue Road. Go about two blocks and look for a sign directing you to Putah Creek Lodge. Turn left at the sign and follow Putah Creek Lodge Road to its end; then park in the gravel lot.

Start bicycling to the west on the asphalt path along the right bank of the creek. The path is wide, smooth, and generally level, but with a few gentle grades. It is well shaded by a variety of trees; indeed, this whole

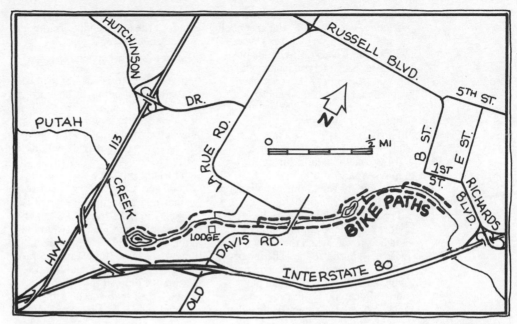

U.C. Davis

ride is through an arboretum. Notice the small wooden posts with signs identifying the trees, bushes, and plantings.

You soon pass the Veterinary Hospital and the Equestrian Center and cross a small dam over the creek. At the dam, the path circles around and leads you to the east along the south bank of the creek. When you get back to the lodge, there is a large lawn and a good picnic area under a grove of California walnut trees.

The path continues to the east. The creek is narrow and shallow here; look for turtles sunning themselves on the rocks. Then, being careful, take the narrow underpass below Old Davis Road.

You are now in the heart of the campus. Cross the creek on one of the graceful curved bridges, follow the

path on the north side past a cactus and succulent garden, and go under Mrak Hall Drive. You then come to a pond bordered by a lawn and crowded with ducks and geese. This is another pleasant place for a picnic.

From the pond, the path on the south side of the creek goes through a cool redwood grove, passes a few more streets on the edge of downtown Davis, and comes to an end at the Southern Pacific tracks. Turn around here and return to Putah Creek Lodge.

There are many other bike paths you can take in the area. There is a whole network of broad paths and closed streets crossing the campus; feel free to try them out. The city also has some wonderful bicycle routes. In particular, you could try the greenbelt through the northern part of town—just park on Alvarado Avenue one block east of Anderson Road and bike for miles through parks, past playgrounds, farmlands, and energy-efficient homes with solar water-heaters on their roofs.

The university offers a one-hour walking tour of the campus at 11:30 and 1:30 on weekends during the academic year and at other times by arrangement. Telephone the Visitor's Office at (916) 752-0539.

The Pena Adobe in Vacaville is a restored Mexican adobe home furnished as it was when the Pena family lived there in the 1840s. The facility includes a museum, picnic grounds, a biking and hiking trail, and a par course. Located off highway I-80 at Pena Adobe Road; open Wednesday through Sunday 9–dusk; free. Telephone (707) 448-8418. Also off I-80 in Vacaville is the Nut Tree, a commercial establishment with a fine restaurant, snack bars, a gift and toy shop, a private airport, a miniature train ride, summer concerts, and a fall pumpkin patch; open daily. Telephone (707) 448-6411.

U.C. Santa Cruz

Distance: 3.6 miles from Old Barn to Upper Quarry and return

Grade level: Difficult

Path condition: Paved; wide, smooth

Topography: Mostly open, deep shade at the north end; hills, quarries, forests, college buildings

Usage: Lightly traveled

U.C. Santa Cruz is one of the newest and most interesting of the University of California campuses. You will enjoy a spectacular ride with panoramic views. But don't bring small children; this is a very difficult ride with a climb of 420 feet.

The land was once part of the 10,000 acre Cowell Ranch. Started as a small quarrying operation by two pioneers in 1849, the land was purchased by Henry Cowell twenty years later. Cowell and his descendants operated a major limestone operation and engaged in logging and cattle raising. In 1955, at the death of S.H. Cowell, the ranch was closed and divided. The U.C. Board of Regents acquired 3,000 acres and opened UCSC in 1965.

The university adopted the collegiate system that has distinguished Oxford University since the thirteenth century and which was later adopted by Yale and Harvard. There are eight villagelike residential colleges, each of which is a small self-contained community of about 700 undergraduates. Each college has its own classrooms, residence halls, dining facility, library, and extracurricular activities but draws on the faculty, academic resources, and physical facilities of the entire campus.

From downtown Santa Cruz, take Bay Drive west to the corner of High Street. Then park in the lot of the Old Barn at the corner. If parking isn't available here, there is a paved lot one block east at the corner of High Street and Cardiff Place.

The Old Barn is a relic of the Cowell Ranch now used as a theater. Many other ranch buildings in weathered wood and fieldstone can be seen in the vicinity. The cookhouse is now the Admissions Office; the granary is a day-care center; the carriage house is used for Receiving and Physical Planning.

The bike path leads to the north on the left side of Glenn Coolidge Drive. You pass the cookhouse and some old lime kilns and then leave the roadside and begin to climb very steeply. You are now passing through the Great Meadow. With the exception of a small stand of fragrant bay trees on your right, the hillside is open, covered with wild grasses and weeds. In the springtime, there are California poppies, lupines, pansies, and yellow mariposas.

After much effort and not much distance, you come to a fork where the trail splits into two one-way paths. The uphill bicyclers bear right here and continue to climb for a short distance. You can now look down on your right into the Lower Quarry. The level section doesn't last very long; there is one more steep upgrade before you reach the main campus.

When you come to the end of the bike path, rest for a while and catch your breath. You may decide you have done enough bicycling and return down the path. If you wish to continue, turn right on the road leading to McHenry Library.

You share the road with light local traffic for 0.2 mile. On this section, you leave the meadow and enter a deep forest of redwood and Douglas fir, with some oak, madrone, maple, and bay trees. At the parking lot, continue to the left up the service road to the library, which is open to the public. The library has a special collections section with Santa Cruz regional history, works of Thomas Carlyle and other materials. The lower courtyard is landscaped with Japanese maples and Australian tree ferns.

From the library, continue along Steinhart Way toward Central Services. The road is closed to private cars; on weekdays during the school year, yellow minibuses pass along it. The buses are free and travel in circular routes around the campus. You soon come to the heart of the campus at the intersection of Steinhart Way and Hagar Drive.

Both the Whole Earth Restaurant, which features natural foods, and the Bay Tree Bookstore are open to the public. The campus information office, in the Redwood Building above the restaurant, has brochures on self-guided walking tours.

Before returning, visit the Upper Quarry. Walk or bike through the parking lot below the bookstore to the quarry. Through the efforts of human beings and nature, this has been turned from an ugly hole in the ground into a quiet, beautiful, tree-lined bowl. University commencements are held here. Behind the stage, an old gravel road leads into the depths of the quarry, where you can see an example of the limestone which contributed to the prosperity of the Cowell Ranch.

When you decide to return, go back past the library to the start of the bike path. On the ride down, you will enjoy an incredible view across Santa Cruz

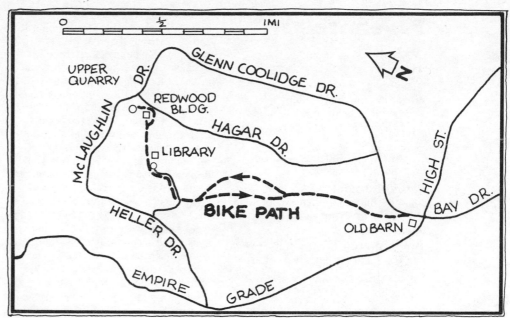

U.C. Santa Cruz

and Monterey Bay. As you go whizzing down the hillside, you will experience one of the finest pleasures of bicycle riding.

A fun activity after your ride is a train ride through the redwoods. The Roaring Camp and Big Trees Railroad in nearby Felton offers excursion rides on a narrow-gauge steam railroad. The grounds feature picnicking, hiking, Western barbecues, and a general store. Open daily except Christmas; trains run Monday through Friday at 12; Saturday and Sunday at 11:00, 12:15, 1:30, 2:45, and 4:00; adults $5.95, children three to fifteen $3.95. Telephone (408) 335-4400.

The Mystery Spot is a ranch in the redwoods north of Santa Cruz at which the laws of gravity are apparently violated. Located at 1953 Branciforte Drive, 4 miles north of town; open daily 9:30–5; adults $2.50, children under twelve $1.25. Telephone (408) 423-8897.

The Santa Cruz beach and boardwalk is an amusement area with roller coasters, merry-go-rounds, arcade games, and the like, located on the beach in downtown Santa Cruz. Open Saturday 11–9, Sunday 10–7, open daily in the summer 11–10; no admission charge, but you pay for the rides. Telephone (408) 423-5590.

The Santa Cruz City Museum has exhibits on local history and Indian culture, and several natural history rooms. Located at 1305 East Cliff Drive; open Tuesday through Saturday 10–5, Sunday 12–5; free. Telephone (408) 429-3773.

Yosemite Valley

Distance: 4.8 miles from Curry Village parking lot to Happy Isles, Mirror Lake, and return via Indian Caves. 7.8 miles to include a side trip to the Visitor Center.

Grade level: Moderate, with one difficult hill at Mirror Lake

Path condition: Paved; wide, smooth, well maintained except near Visitor Center, where it is narrow and rough

Topography: Shady; forests, rivers, meadows, granite cliffs, waterfalls

Usage: Varies from light to heavy depending on time of day and time of year

Like a child organizing his dinner, I have saved the best for last. A bicycle trip in Yosemite National Park is an incomparable family experience. Because the roads in the eastern end of Yosemite Valley have been closed to automobile traffic, you will be able to enjoy the scenery while you ride. And what scenery! If you have been there, you will know all about the magnificent cliffs, waterfalls, and meadows in this glacier-carved wonderland. If you have never been there, by all means plan a trip.

Spring and fall are the best seasons for a Yosemite bicycle trip. The waterfalls are at their fullest in late spring and early summer. And the changing colors of the foliage make the park particularly beautiful in the autumn. Yosemite is notorious for overcrowding and traffic jams during summer vacation; however, I believe this reputation is exaggerated. If you avoid the Independence Day and Labor Day weekends, you will probably find that, though there are a lot of people around, the situation is quite tolerable.

There are a number of good motels and lodges on the outskirts of the park at El Portal and Fish Camp, but I recommend staying in Yosemite Valley. It is a long, difficult drive into the valley; you don't want to take it more often than necessary. Make reservations well in advance at the elegant Ahwanee Hotel, comfortable Yosemite Lodge, or the more spartan accommodations at Camp Curry; telephone (209) 373-4171. Camping in the Valley is by reservation only between May and October; reservations may be made up to eight weeks in advance through Ticketron outlets. Campgrounds are either closed or on a first-come first-served basis the rest of the year.

Begin the bike ride from the large parking lot at Curry Village. If you haven't brought your own bike, one-speed bikes may be rented for $1.50 an hour at Curry Village or Yosemite Lodge. Walk your bikes toward the main buildings and then turn left on the road right in front of them. This road carries light local traffic for 0.1 mile. If you don't want to ride along with traffic, you could walk your bikes on this section or ride on the narrow, paved sidewalk.

Soon you see a sign directing all motorized traffic to turn left. Continue to the right on the road, which is

Yosemite Valley

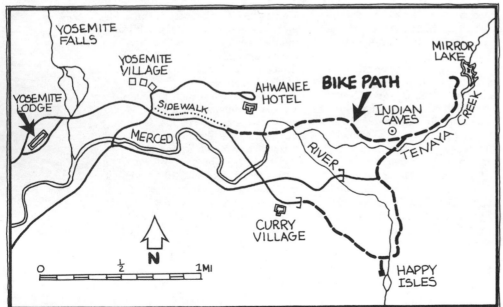

reserved for bicycles and shuttle buses only. The road is very wide and smooth; a campground is on your left and a forest of Ponderosa and Jeffrey pine, Douglas fir, and Sierra redwood on your right. The road climbs gradually uphill to Happy Isles.

Park your bikes and spend some time at Happy Isles. There are restrooms, a bike rack, and a concession stand here. The Trail Center has several exhibits and presents slide shows on the birds, animals, and trails of Yosemite. The friendly rangers will be happy to answer your questions and to provide suggestions for hiking. The Trail Center is open from 10 to 4 daily in the summer and on weekends during the rest of the year. Happy Isles is the trailhead for a number of hiking trails, including the very popular steep trail to Vernal and Nevada falls. Even if you don't plan to hike, spend a few minutes walking around the isles. The many branches of the river tumbling noisily past rocks, laced by walking bridges, and forested with conifers, maple, oak, and dogwood make this a delightful place to stroll and forget your cares—it's easy to understand the name of the area after just a short time here.

After leaving Happy Isles, return to the road, cross the bridge over the Merced River, and follow the road along the east bank. Looking ahead, you have fine views of North Dome, Washington Column, and the Royal Arches. You soon come to a fork where the shuttle buses turn left toward the stables and Camp Curry. Turn right here; you now have to share the road only with walkers.

Cross the Tenaya Bridge and bear right at the junction of the bicycle path to Indian Caves. Now you come

to the one steep part of the ride, a climb of 120 feet to Mirror Lake; you may want to walk your bikes up this hill. On your right is the beautiful maple-lined bank of the rapidly thundering Tenaya Creek. At the top of the hill are a bike rack, water, and restrooms.

Mirror Lake was created by an accidental rock fall which dammed the rapids of Tenaya Creek late in the nineteenth century. Because of the dramatic effect mirroring Half Dome, the National Park Service decided to maintain the lake. This involved dredging the lake for silt and depositing additional rocks at the dam as necessary. In 1971, the NPS decided to stop interfering with nature. Now each year a new load of sand is washed down from the mountains, and the lake gets progressively smaller. A sign informs visitors that they are watching the birth of Mirror Meadow.

You may enjoy a wade in the shallow part of the lake. The water is very cold all year, and only a few brave souls actually swim here. Mirror Lake is also a trailhead—an easy 3 mile loop through Tenaya Canyon and Snow Creek Falls as well as a rugged trail to Tenaya Lake and Tuolumne Meadows starts here.

On leaving the lake, note the sign warning you how many people were hurt last summer bicycling down this steep hill. Please be very careful on the downgrade and watch out for people who don't look where they're walking.

At the foot of the hill, bear right on the bicycle path to Indian Caves. The caves are a tremendous network of huge granite boulders. Kids love to climb them and to explore all the nooks and crannies.

At this point, you may have had enough bicycling for one day. If so, return to Curry Village by the shuttle bus road past Happy Isles. Otherwise, continue west on the bicycle path. The path is a wide, smooth, well maintained route going gently downhill through the forest. You cross two stone bridges over the Merced River. It's probably illegal and definitely dangerous, but some bigger kids use these bridges as giant diving boards. Many other people are enjoyably floating down the river on rubber rafts.

Continue past the campground until you reach the main road linking Yosemite Village and Curry Village. You have now come to the end of the good section of the path, and you have four choices for completing your ride. You can turn back and return by the bicycle path to Indian Caves and then by the shuttle bus road past Happy Isles back to Curry Village. Or, if you don't mine riding with traffic for 0.6 mile, you can turn left and take the road directly back to Curry Village. Or you can extend your ride by proceeding either to the Ahwanee Hotel or to Yosemite Village.

Should you choose to go to the Ahwanee, simply take the dirt path across the edge of the meadow to your right. The Ahwanee, which was opened in 1927, is an impressive building constructed of large stones interspersed with massive beams. It has a comfortable large sitting room with picture windows and an immense stone fireplace. The elegant dining room features fine food served in a traditional candlelight setting. Reservations and proper dress (coat and tie for men; dress or pantsuit for women) are required for dinner.

Should you choose to go to Yosemite Village, continue straight ahead from the end of the bike path. You will be on a narrow sidewalk path with open meadows on both sides. The view here is awe inspiring. On your right are the Royal Arches, on your left are Glacier Point and Sentinel Dome, and straight ahead is Upper Yosemite Falls. At the edge of the meadow, the sidewalk path ends at the bridge over Indian Canyon Creek. Now walk or ride your bikes on the road the short additional distance to Yosemite Village.

The businesses at the Village include a grocery store, several restaurants, gift shops, studios, a bank, and a post office. Within walking distance is the Visitor Center, which has a number of fine displays of the geology of Yosemite; open daily 8–7 in summer, shorter hours the rest of the year; telephone (209) 372-4461. Immediately behind the Visitor Center is the Indian Cultural Museum, which has a self-guiding reconstruction of an Ahwaneechee Indian village; open daily in summer 9–12:45 and 2–5:30. After wandering around here, return to your car by way of Indian Caves and Happy Isles.

There are many, many things to do at Yosemite. You can hike, swim, raft, ride horses or mules, or take a guided tour. Telephone or write the Yosemite Park and Curry Company; Yosemite National Park, CA 95389; telephone (209) 372-4611; or Superintendent; Yosemite National Park, CA 95389; telephone (209) 372-4461 for more information.

You can ride the free open-air double-decker shuttle buses around the Valley or take a scenic drive to Glacier Point, Hetch Hetchy Reservoir, Tuolumne Meadows, or the Mariposa Grove of Big Trees. The more ambitious visitor can take a one or two-day course in alpine survival or rock climbing—telephone the Yosemite Mountaineering School at (209) 372-4611, extension 244, for cost, schedule, and reservations.

Index

Alameda County, 13, 16, 19–29, 31
Alameda Creek Equestrian Center, 22
Alameda Creek Trail, 19, 20–22
Alcatraz Island, 46, 62
Alemany, Archbishop, 35
Alexander Lindsay Junior Museum, 37
Alpine Road, 67, 68–70
Alum Rock Park, 79, 80–82
American Association of University
  Women (AAUW), 17
American River Parkway, 93, 94, 95–97
Amusement rides, 14, 25, 28, 38, 41, 60,
  71, 96, 100, 101, 105
Angel Island, 15, 43, 44–46, 52
Angel Island State Park Ferries, 15, 45
Archery, 22, 25, 35, 37, 60, 72
Audubon Canyon Ranch, 50
Ayala, Don Juan Manuel, 45

Balclutha, 62
BART, 15, 21, 25, 41
Bayfront Trail, 67, 70–71, 72
Benicia Capitol State Park, 41

Bicycle World, 16
Bicycling, 16
Billy Jones Steam Railroad, 89
Black Diamond Mines Regional Park, 34
Blackie's Pasture, 52, 53
Boat rentals, 25, 26, 28, 29, 36, 49, 60, 62,
  71, 89, 98, 101, 102
Boat rides, 15, 25, 28, 41, 45–46, 62, 100
Bol Park, 79, 82–84
Botanic Garden, 38
Boyd Science Museum, 48
Brannan Island State Recreation Area, 34
Briones Regional Park, 32, 37
Broderick, David, 63
Buelna, Felix, 69
Burbank, Luther, 102
Bus rides, 15, 40, 52, 105, 108

California Academy of Sciences, 58, 59
California Almond Exchange, 97
California Aqueduct, 93, 94, 97–99

California Exposition, 95
California Railway Museum, 34, 40
CALTRANS, 15, 44, 48, 50, 55, 93
Camron-Stanford House, 27
Canada Road, 67, 71–72, 74
Cannery, 62
Casa de Fruta, 99
Castle Golf And Games, 71
Castro Point Railway Museum, 40
Chabot Queen, 25
Chabot, Anthony, 24
Cheese Factory, 29, 51
Children's Fairyland, 28
Children's Playground, 60
China Camp State Park, 49
Cliff House, 58
Concannon Vineyards, 29
Conservatory, 60
Contra Costa County, 13, 16, 19, 31–41
Contra Loma Regional Park, 31, 32–34, 40
Corte Madera Creek, 43, 46–48
Coutts, Peter, 87

Cowell, Henry, 104
Coyote Creek, 79, 84–85
Coyote Hills Park, 19, 22–23
Coyote Point Museum, 73
Coyote Point Park, 67, 72–74

de Young Museum, 58, 59
Doll Museum, 41
Doss, Margot Patterson, 16, 21
Drawbridge, 23
Dutton, Davis, 17

Eargle, Dolan, 16
East Bay Municipal Utility District
    (EBMUD), 24, 25, 31, 32, 37
East Bay Regional Park District (EBRPD),
    16, 19, 21, 24, 29, 31, 34, 38, 39
Eastridge, 85
Enchanted World of San Francisco, 62
Environmental Education Center, 38
Escalle's, 47
Exploratorium, 60, 61

Fairyland, 28
Fairytale Town, 96
Feliz, Domingo, 75
Ferry rides, 15, 44, 45–46, 53, 62
Filoli, 72
Fire Department Museum, 58
Fisherman's Wharf, 15, 45, 62
Fishing, 15, 24, 25, 29, 34, 36, 40, 49, 51,
    53, 61, 70, 84, 88, 89, 97, 101
Fitzgerald Marine Reserve, 63
Foothill College, 84
Fort Funston, 63
Fort Mason, 55, 60–61
Fort Point, 57, 58, 60
Fremont Central Park, 22, 25
Frenchman's Hill, 79, 84, 85–87

General Motors, 26
Ghirardelli Square, 62
Gibson Ranch County Park, 96
Golden Gate Bridge, 38, 45, 55, 56–58, 60,
    96
Golden Gate National Recreation Area
    (GGNRA), 38, 43, 55, 56, 57, 58, 60, 61
Golden Gate Park, 55, 58–60, 63, 64
Golden Gate Promenade, 45, 55, 58, 60–62
Golden Gate Transit, 15, 57
Guide Dogs for the Blind, 49

Hall, William, 58
Happy Hollow Children's Park, 82
Haraszthy, Count, 75
Harbor Carriers, 15, 45, 62
Hellyer Park, 84
Hershey's chocolate, 98
Hetch Hetchy system, 72, 76, 80, 83, 108
Hiking, 16, 22, 23, 25, 34, 35, 37, 49, 50,
    51, 52, 53, 58, 72, 77, 87, 100, 104, 107,
    108
Hill Country, 85
Horse rides, 22, 25, 38, 108
Houseboats, 50
Howarth Park, 100, 101
Huddart Park, 72
Hyde Street Pier, 62

Indian villages, 22, 23, 52, 108

Jack London Square, 28
Jackson, Joan, 16
James V. Fitzgerald Marine Reserve, 63
Japanese Tea Gardens, 58, 60, 75, 82
Jewel Lake, 38
John Muir National Historic Site, 41
Josephine Randall Junior Museum, 64
Junior League, 17
Junipero Serra County Park, 77

Kaiser Center, 27
Kennedy Park, 25

Lafayette-Moraga Trail, 31, 34–35
Lafayette Reservoir, 31, 36–37
Lake Anza, 38
Lake Chabot, 19, 24–25
Lake Elizabeth, 19, 25–26
Lake Merced, 55, 62–63
Lake Merritt, 19, 26–28
Lake Tahoe Bikeway, 93, 94, 99–100
Lakeside Park Garden Center, 28
Lane Publishers, 70
Lawrence Hall of Science, 39
Lawrence Livermore Lab, 29
Lewis, Mary and Richard, 17
Lick Observatory, 82
Lick, James, 60
Lindsay Junior Museum, 37

Little Farm, 38
Livermore Bikepath, 19, 28–29
London, Jack, 28, 102
Los Gatos Creek, 79, 87–89
Louise Boyd Museum of Science, 48

Margolin, Malcolm, 16
Marin Art and Garden Center, 47
Marin County, 13, 15, 16, 43–53, 56, 57,
    58, 60, 61, 93
Marin County Civic Center, 49
Marin County Heliport, 50
Marin Headlands, 58
Marin Miwok Museum, 51
Marine World, 70, 71
Marinship, 50
Marksmanship ranges, 25, 62, 73
McLaren, John, 58
Merritt Queen, 28
Merritt, Sam, 27
Midpeninsula Regional Open Space
    District, 87
Miller's California Ranch, 98
Mission Dolores, 65
Mission San Jose, 26
Mission San Rafael, 48
Miwok Indians, 51
Miwok Park, 50, 51
Model trains, 37, 64
Moffett Field, 84
Morrison Planetarium, 59
Motorland, 16
Mount Diablo State Park, 35
Mount Tamalpais State Park, 44, 50
Muir Beach, 50
Muir Woods National Monument, 50
Muir, John, 41
Murphy, Tom, 16
Musee Mecanique, 58
Mystery Spot, 105

NASA/Ames Research Center, 84
National Maritime Museum, 62
New Almaden Museum, 85
Newey, Bob, 16
Nike Missile Sites, 22, 23, 37, 38, 45, 46,
    58
Niles, 21
Nimitz Way, 31, 37–39
Nut Tree, 104

Oakland Municipal Auditorium, 27
Oakland Museum, 27, 28
Oakland Zoo, 25
Oakwood Lake Resort, 98
Ocean Beach, 63
Ohlone Indians, 23
Old Sacramento, 97
Old St. Hilary's Historic Preserve, 53
Orchard RV Park, 98
Osio, Antonio Mario, 45

Pacific flyway, 22, 39
Palo Alto Baylands Interpretive Center, 87
Palo Alto Junior Museum, 91
Par courses, 25, 35, 47, 52, 61, 62, 87, 88, 101, 104
Paradise Beach County Park, 53
Pena Adobe, 104
Percolation ponds, 84, 85, 88
Petaluma Adobe State Historical Monument, 52
Pier 39, 62
Pilgreen, Tedi, 17
Pixie Playland, 41
Point Pinole, 31, 39–40
Point Reyes National Seashore, 44, 52, 64
Polk, Willis, 72
Polo Field, 59, 63, 64
Pomada, Elizabeth, 17
Ponderosa Ranch, 100
Port Chicago Highway, 31, 40–41
Port Costa, 41
Pulgas Water Temple, 72

Ralston Cutoff, 67, 72, 74–75
Ralston, William, 75
Randall Junior Museum, 64
Redwood Empire Ice Arena, 102
Redwood Highway, 43, 48–49
Redwood Regional Park, 35
Richardson Bay Wildlife Sanctuary, 53
Richmond Museum, 40
Ripley, Robert, 62, 102
River Ranch Lodge, 99–100
Roaring Camp and Big Trees Railroad, 105
Rod McLellan Company, 74
Romero Visitor Center, 98
Rosicrucian Museum and Planetarium, 89
Ross, Thomas and Carol, 16
Rotary Natural Science Center, 28

Roth, Lillian Matson, 72
Ryan Lab, 86

San Francisco Airport, 73, 74
San Francisco Bay Model, 50
San Francisco Bay Wildlife Refuge, 23
San Francisco County, 13, 55–65
San Francisco Zoo, 64
San Jose Historical Museum, 82
San Jose Zoo, 82
San Mateo Central Park, 75
San Mateo County, 13, 67–77
San Mateo County Historical Museum, 75, 77
Sanchez Adobe, 63
Santa Clara County, 13, 79–91
Santa Cruz Beach and Boardwalk, 105
Santa Cruz City Museum, 105
Sausalito Bikeway, 43, 45, 49–50
Sawyer's Camp Road, 67, 75–77
Sawyer, Leander, 76
Schulz, Charles, 102
Schussler, Herman, 76
Shadow Cliffs Regional Recreation Area, 29
Sierra Club, 16
Sonoma State Historic Park, 102
Splashdown, 26
Spring Lake Park, 93, 94, 100–102
St. Mary's College, 35
Stafford Lake, 43, 50–52
Standing, Tom, 16
Stanford Linear Accelerator, 70
Stanford University, 79, 84, 86, 87, 89–91
Stanford, Leland, 87, 89–90
State Capitol, 95, 96
State Indian Museum, 96
Stateline Fire Lookout, 100
Steinhart Aquarium, 59
Stinson Beach, 50, 58
Stony Ridge Winery, 29
Stow Lake, 59, 60
Strauss, Joseph, 57
Stream Profile Chamber, 100
Strybing Arboretum, 60
Sulphur Creek Park, 22
Sunol Regional Park, 22
Sunset Bikeway, 55, 63–65
Sunset magazine, 16, 70
Sutter's Fort, 96
Swimming, 26, 29, 33–34, 35, 37, 38, 50, 53, 73, 98, 102, 108

Tabe, Tom, 16
Teather, Louise, 16
Terry, David, 63
Thornton State Beach, 63
Tiburon Bikeway, 43, 45, 52–53
Tiburon Uplands Natural Preserve, 53
Tilden Park, 37–39
Tours, 14, 26, 27, 29, 34, 49, 62, 70, 74, 75, 84, 88, 96, 97, 98, 100, 102
Train rides, 15, 25, 34, 38, 40, 41, 75, 89, 99, 102, 104, 105
Train Town, 102
Triple Pines Ranch, 25
Truckee River rafting, 99–100

U.S. Navy at Moffett Field, 84
U.S. Weather Bureau, 74
University of California, Davis, 93, 94, 102–104
University of California, Santa Cruz, 82, 93, 94, 104–105

Vallejo Flour Mill Historic Park, 20
Vallejo, Jose, 20
Vallejo, Mariano, 52, 102
Vasona Lake Park, 89
Velodrome, 84
Vikingsholm, 100
Villa Armando Winery, 29

Walnut Creek Model Railroaders, 37
Water slides, 26, 71, 98
Wattis Hall of Man, 59
Wente Brothers, 29
Whitnah, Dorothy, 16
Wildflower nature trail, 37
Wildlife refuges, 23, 28, 53
William Land Park, 96
Winchester Mystery House, 88
Winchester, Sarah, 88
Wine tasting, 29, 99
Wonder Bread, 97
Woodside Store Museum, 72
Wright, Frank Lloyd, 49

Yosemite Valley, 93, 94, 106–108
Youth Science Institute (YSI), 81–82, 89

Zoos, 25, 64, 73, 82, 96, 99